Sweet abalone can be found
Upon its rocky shore
While crabs and salmon both abound
And juicy albacore.
Before I tire; ere you go
I would propose a toast:
"We found it clean — let's keep it so"
The Mendocino Coast.

— conclusion of anonymous poem reprinted with permission from
the Mendocino Beacon.

The HIKER'S hip pocket GUIDE to the Mendocino Coast

by
Bob Lorentzen

BORED FEET PUBLICATIONS
MENDOCINO, CALIFORNIA
1986

Illustrations by Joshua Edelman
Symbols by Jann Patterson-Watters and Taylor Cranney
Maps by Bob Lorentzen
Designed by Judy Detrick

Published by
Bored Feet Publications
Post Office Box 1832
Mendocino, California 95460
(707) 964-6629

Library of Congress Cataloging-in-Publication Data
Lorentzen, Bob, 1949-
    The hiker's hip pocket guide to the Mendocino coast.

    Bibliography: p. 169.
    Includes index.
    1. Hiking—California—Mendocino County—
Guide-books.
2. Mendocino County (Calif.)—Description and travel—Guide-books. I. Title.
GV199.42 C22M464 1986   917.94'15 86-30960

ISBN 0-939431-00-9 Softcover.

10 9 8 7 6 5 4 3 2

DEDICATED TO MY GRANDPARENTS:

Sam Harman (Pal), a fly fisherman and gardener extraordinaire who showed me the fine points of nature.

Eris Rasmussen Harman, hiker and early member of the Wasatch Mountain Club, whose spirit soars with the music of nature.

Eden Christian Lorentzen, fisherman and gardener, who gave me his explorer's blood, took me fishing and baited my hook until I had the stomach to do it myself.

Ruth Blake Lorentzen, teacher, poet and saint.

This book is also dedicated to the prospect of no oil exploration or drilling off the shore of the Mendocino Coast. Save the coast for future generations.

ACKNOWLEDGMENTS

I am most grateful to everyone involved in the creation of this book. In particular I wish to thank: Patricia Priano, my treasured partner, for her encouragement from initial seed to final fruition, reasonable patience with the miniscule details of the creative process, and most of all, her confidence in me; Judy Detrick for her early encouragement, continuing perseverance and remarkable design talents; Joshua Edelman for his commitment to producing the fine illustrations and his sense of humor; Jann Patterson-Watters for her marvelous symbols, enthusiasm and infectious excitement; Amanda Avery for her critical and objective editing; Margaret Fox for her acumen in editing and marketing and her willingness to believe in this book when it had not yet been created; Carole Raye, Peter Sherman, Janis Appier, Charles Peterson and Carolyn Lorentzen, my mother, for their incisive editing and pithy feedback; Anthony Miksak, Linda Pack and Ruth Dobberpuhl of the Gallery Bookshop for their understanding, patience and book sense; May, China and Leilani Edelman, Jeffrey Garcia, Ray and Marsha Smith, David Springer, Maryellen Sheppard and Christopher Kump for testing trails and helping to decide what works; Sue Miles of the Mendocino Area State Parks, Tom Sutphen of Jackson State Forest, John Jennings of the Sinkyone, Mark Rawitsch of Mendocino County Museum, and everyone at the Kelley House for providing valuable information; Randy Bancroft for his positive attitude and fine tuning adjustments; Taylor Cranney for her help with the symbols; Karl and Jane Lorentzen, Gina Salamone, Judith Becker and all of the other people who have provided encouragement, enthusiasm and help.

With special thanks to Sam O. Watnick for teaching me to cruise timber and providing a model for hope and determination.

And with apologies and thanks to Ed Abbey for all his passionate and inspiring writings about experiencing, loving and saving the natural world.

CONTENTS

INTRODUCTION

THIS BOOK IS FOR RECREATIONAL PURPOSES ONLY

Highway 1 curves and twists for 105 miles along the Mendocino Coast. It provides access, mostly close at hand, to 131 miles of rugged shoreline. This isolated coast, with its many scattered pocket beaches, is backed by approximately 1000 square miles of forest (and cutover timber land), an intricate labyrinth of ridges, canyons and valleys, through which no less than 7 rivers and dozens of creeks flow west into the sea. At its northern end, Highway 1 veers inland and meets its northern terminus at Leggett on Highway 101. But the coast continues north to its most isolated wilderness stretch: Sinkyone Wilderness State Park and King Range Conservation Area — the Lost Coast.

This book tells how to find and walk, hike, jog or ride over 200 miles of scenic trails through this beautiful country. The trails range from easy walks to difficult backpacks, with emphasis on easy trails and day hikes. The trails lead to a variety of habitats: beaches, tidepools, lagoons, dunes, headlands, forests, stream canyons, ridges and mountain tops. You may also hike trails to waterfalls and ghost towns, along old logging railways, through a beautiful cultivated garden, or take a history tour of Mendocino, Fort Bragg or the Point Arena lighthouse. In short, there is something for everyone. So get out of your car and use feet, bicycle, horse or wheelchair to explore the Mendocino Coast.

HOW TO USE THIS BOOK

The trails in this book are organized from the north to the south. Except for the northernmost group of trails, all trails are organized along the length of Highway 1. They are no more than one hour from Mendocino or Fort Bragg.

In the directions to each trail you will find a milepost number on Highway 1, listed like this: M.49.88. These refer to the white highway mileposts which are placed frequently (but at irregular intervals) along Highway 1 by CalTrans, the State Department of Transportation. Though this book gives more complete directions to each trailhead, you may quickly determine the location of a trail (and where it is in relation to you) by referring to its milepost number.

There is no need to start at the beginning of the book. Simply turn to the trail nearest your location and you will be on your way. Other trails nearby will be on the adjacent pages.

For each trail in the book you will find a map, specific directions to the trailhead, the best time to go, appropriate warnings, and a detailed trail description which includes a bit of history and/or natural history.

Below the access information for each trail you will also find a group of symbols. They tell you at a glance the level of difficulty, the type of trail, what facilities are available, whether there is a fee, and whether dogs are allowed. The list of symbols follows.

At the end of the book are appendixes which list the trails most suitable for a particular type of recreation: bicycles, mountain bikes, equestrians, backpacking trails and trails accessible to the handicapped. The appendixes also have information on where you can put your canoe in the water along the rivers of the Mendocino Coast and where you can assuage your voracious hunger after that hike at one of the author's favorite restaurants along the coast. There is also an index and a selected bibliography.

THE SYMBOLS

WALK:
Less than 2 miles
Easy terrain

EASY HIKE:
2 to 10 miles
Easy terrain

MODERATE HIKE:
2 to 10 miles
Rougher terrain

DIFFICULT HIKE:
Strenuous terrain
Backpacking possible

**MOUNTAIN BIKE
TRAIL**

PICNIC SPOT:
May be tables or just
a good blanket spot

BIKE TRAIL

**DOGS ALLOWED
ON LEASH**

CAR CAMPING

**WALK-IN OR
BIKE-IN CAMPING:**
Environmental camps

TIDEPOOL ACCESS

HANDICAP ACCESS

RECOMMENDED
FOR FAMILIES

INTERPRETIVE
NATURE TRAIL

TRAIL FOR
EQUESTRIANS

RESTROOMS
AVAILABLE

WATER AVAILABLE

FEE AREA

FISHING ACCESS

NO OIL EXPLORATION
OR DRILLING

THE DANGERS
TEN COASTAL COMMANDMENTS

When on the trail, *always* keep your senses wide open. Don't let nature lull you into total complacency. In this way you can best appreciate nature's pleasures, as well as her dangers. Here are ten rules to keep you out of danger, so that you may safely enjoy the beauty of the coast.

1. DON'T LITTER. Most of these places are unspoiled. Do your part to keep them that way. Always hike with a trash bag and use it, even for matches, cigarette butts and bottle caps. I always pick up any trash I see in a pristine spot, my way of saying thanks to Mother Nature.

2. NO TRESPASSING. Property owners have a right to privacy. Stay off private property. There are enough public places without walking through someone's front or back yard.

3. NEVER TURN YOUR BACK ON THE OCEAN. Oversized, rogue waves can strike the coast at any time. They are especially common in winter. They have killed people; watch for them. More subtle are the changes of the tides: don't let rising tides strand you against steep cliffs or on a submerged tidal island. The ocean is icy and unforgiving, generally unsafe for swimming without a wetsuit.

4. STAY BACK FROM CLIFFS. Coastal soils are often unstable. You wouldn't want to fall 40 feet into the icy sea, would you? Don't get too close to the cliff's edge and never climb on cliffs unless there is a safe trail.

5. WILD THINGS: ANIMAL. All the animal pests of the Mendocino Coast are small, unless you get chased by a Roosevelt elk (generally they will not chase you if you do not run). Watch out for ticks, wasps, mosquitoes, biting spiders, scorpions and rattlesnakes. Human animals are easily the most dangerous, especially in deer hunting season (from the first week in August until the end of September). Always listen for gunfire, especially outside state parks. *Never* (even in a vehicle) enter an area where logging is in progress. UNDERWATER ANIMALS: When tide pooling or at the beach always watch for sea urchins and jellyfish. Both have stinging spines which are quite painful. Remember, too, that mussels

are quarantined each year from May through October: at that time they contain deadly poison.

6. WILD THINGS: PLANT. These mean business too, especially poison oak and stinging nettles which can get you with the slightest touch. Many other plants are poisonous. It is best to not touch any plants unless you know by positive identification that they are safe; this is most important with mushrooms.

poison oak

7. POT GARDENS. Don't even think about messing with one, no matter whose side you are on. If you ever stumble onto a pot patch, leave more quietly than you came. Take only memories.

8. TRAFFIC. Coast roads are difficult and often overcrowded. Drive carefully and courteously. Please turn out for faster traffic. You will enjoy the coast more if you do. If you stop, pull safely off the road.

9. CRIME. Be sure to lock your car when you leave it at the trailhead. Leave valuables out of sight, or better yet, back at your lodging.

10. ALWAYS TAKE RESPONSIBILITY FOR YOURSELF AND YOUR PARTY. This is a trail guide, not a nursery school. The author cannot and will not be responsible for you in the wilds. Informa-

tion contained in this book is correct to the best of the author's knowledge. Author and publisher assume no liability for damages arising from errors or omissions. You must take the responsibility for your safety and health while on these trails. The coast is still a wild place. Safety conditions of trails, beaches and tidepools vary with seasons and tides. Be cautious, heed the above warnings and always check on local conditions. It is always better to hike with a friend. Know where the nearest help can be found if an emergency should arise.

THE HISTORY

The Mendocino Coast was born about 40 million years ago, the result of the collision of two giant pieces of the earth's crust (tectonic plates). As the North American plate moved substantially westward, it collided with and overrode the Pacific plate. The Coast Ranges were built by the sedimentary material scraped from the Pacific plate in this process. Though the collision became more gentle over the ensuing eons, the plates continue to collide today. Over the last million years, a series of five to seven marine terraces have been successively uplifted, each one serving its time as the sea coast before being lifted above sea level. This process has occurred most regularly, creating a complex and fascinating natural history which is repeated nowhere else in the world. You can see evidence of this process at many places on the Mendocino Coast, but the best classroom is the Jughandle Ecological Staircase (trail #18).

The San Andreas Fault now forms the dividing line between the two tectonic plates. The San Andreas runs north into the ocean near Manchester, then continues offshore to Cape Mendocino. The Pacific plate, to the west of the fault, began to move northward about 25 million years ago.

Two distinct plant groups mingle here on the Mendocino Coast. Plants of a cooler, wetter climate migrated from the north. These include redwood, fir and tanoak. Representatives of the drier, warmer climate of the south include madrone, manzanita, bay laurel, Bishop pine and ceanothus.

Archeological evidence taken from shell mounds shows that Native Americans lived along the coast for at least 4000 years before the settlers came. Their relatively simple culture prospered with California's abundant natural resources until the coming of the white settlers.

The first Spanish galleon is believed to have sailed along the Mendocino Coast about 1543. The ship's captain named Cape Mendocino, in Humboldt County, in honor of the Viceroy of New Spain, Don Antonio de Mendoza. Though galleons sailed the coast into the 1800s, there was never any record of a landing in what is now Mendocino County.

The Russians also had their time along the coast, establishing Fort Ross (in Sonoma County) in 1812. The Russian fur trappers had been working along the coast even before this time. The name Russian Gulch originated because the Native Americans told of seeing white men there with a large ship. From the Natives' descriptions, the white men were Russian fur trappers; the date was in the late eighteenth century. Having exhausted the fur trade, the Russians abandoned the coast in 1841.

With the coming of the California gold rush, beginning in 1848, Americans began to explore the north coast, seeking timber and other resources to supply California's booming growth. Albion, Greenwood and Mendocino were among the first settlements. By 1900 there were more than three dozen towns on the Mendocino Coast, all connected to the timber trade. The tiny mill towns and ports came and went, but by 1940 fifty sawmills were scattered on the Coast. A postwar boom increased the number to 129 mills. Then improved roads and modernization caused the mills to be consolidated. By 1960, only three mills remained. Only a dozen of the towns remain today. As you read about the trails and hike along the coast, many details of the coast's history will fall into place.

THE CLIMATE

The climate of the Mendocino Coast is mild enough that you may hike year-round, if you are prepared for varying conditions. In planning your excursions, keep in mind the following about the seasons along the Mendocino Coast:

16

November to March are the rainy months, time to bring rain coats and rubber boots. Still, there are often fine sunny days between storms.

April and May are often windy, with occasional rain storms. The wind may be gentle, or fierce and unrelenting. The landscape is at its most lush and beautiful. Bring layered clothing and hats.

June, July and August bring sunny summer days, alternating with thick fog. You may be comfortable in shorts, but bring layered clothing in case the fog comes in. Sometimes you can beat the fog by heading a few miles inland. (This is the most crowded season, especially August.)

September and October are a beautiful time. Fog is less common. Though there may be rainstorms, most of the days are calm and warm. The land is dry, the hills are golden, and the sunsets are often spectacular.

GET READY, GET SET, HIKE!

You should be chomping at the bit to get out on the trail by now. Here are a few suggestions of what you might need to take on your hike: layered clothing — sweater, sweatshirt, hat, windbreaker or rain coat; insect repellent; suntan lotion; sunglasses; and small first aid kit (at least bring moleskin for blisters). Not essential, but highly recommended for all but the shortest walks: water container, extra food, pocket knife, flashlight and extra batteries, matches and fire starter, map, compass (helps if you know how to use it), and of course you would not want to be caught without your *Hip Pocket Guide!*

Additional suggestions: camera; dry socks; binoculars; and field guide to birds, wildflowers and/or trees. If you are backpacking you should consult an equipment list for that purpose.

When you are out on the trails, remember to slow down, open your senses and enjoy. Most people hike at a rate of 2 to 3 miles per hour. But beach sand or steep terrain may slow all but the most hardy to as little as one mile per hour. Leave ample time to do the hike you plan at a pleasant pace. Hike not to count the miles, but for the enjoyment and appreciation of nature. Happy trails to you!

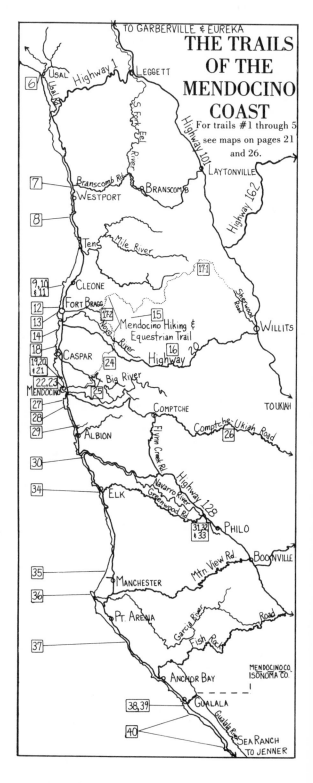

TO GARBERVILLE & EUREKA

THE TRAILS
OF THE
MENDOCINO
COAST

For trails #1 through 5
see maps on pages 21
and 26.

6

Usal

Highway 1

LEGGETT

S. Fork Eel River

Highway 101

LAYTONVILLE

Highway 162

7

Branscomb Rd.

WESTPORT

BRANSCOMB

8

Ten Mile River

9,10 & 11

CLEONE

17·1

12

FORT BRAGG

Sherwood Road

WILLITS

13

17·2

15

Mendocino Hiking & Equestrian Trail

14

Noyo River

18

16

Highway 20

19,20 & 21

CASPAR

24

22,23

Big River

MENDOCINO

25

27

COMPTCHE

TO UKIAH

28

29

Comptche-Ukiah Road

26

ALBION

30

Flynn Creek Rd.

Highway 128

34

ELK

Navarro River

Greenwood Rd.

31,32 & 33

PHILO

Mtn. View Rd.

BOONVILLE

35

MANCHESTER

36

PT. ARENA

Garcia River

Road

37

Fish Rock

MENDOCINO CO.
SONOMA CO.

ANCHOR BAY

38,39

GUALALA

Gualala River

40

SEA RANCH

TO JENNER

18

1

CHEMISE MOUNTAIN

GREAT VIEWS OF THE COAST

This well-engineered trail climbs up the wooded side of an otherwise brushy mountain to commanding views up and down the coast and over the surrounding countryside. This is the southern end of the King Range Conservation Area.

Your trail starts at the pleasantly wooded campground, crossing a small bridge over Bear Creek. Just 150 feet beyond the bridge is the small King Range Nature Trail on the right, wandering near the creek. Beyond the junction you start to climb, crossing two small tributaries which may be flowing in spring. Sword ferns grow on the north-facing slope beneath a mature fir forest. Salal and huckleberry grow on the drier south-facing slope.

Continue the steady climb for 1/4 mile to the junction with the trail from Nadelos Campground. Just beyond the junction you will find a trail register. Sign in, please. Your trail steepens for the next 1/8 mile. Then the ridgetop looms ahead. You switchback to the left and meet the Hidden Valley spur trail, branching to the right. (This leads generally north along the ridge, returning to the Chemise Mountain Road near the junction with the Shelter Cove Road.) Take the left fork.

Your climb becomes more gradual as you head south just below the ridgetop. The mixed conifer forest changes to predominantly hardwoods. About one mile from the trailhead your trail levels. The snow-covered Yolla Bolly mountains appear through the trees to the east. In 1/8 mile you top the ridge, but tall brush conceals the views. Another 1/8 mile beyond, the brush parts for a view of Shelter Cove to the northwest.

Just 1 3/8 miles from the trailhead, a sign marks the 2596-foot summit on your left. A narrow, overgrown trail winds to the very top in about 150 feet. The side trip is worthwhile, as the brush parts sufficiently to divulge the fine views in all directions. From the summit a few houses are visible nearby.

CHEMISE MOUNTAIN:

DISTANCE: 2 3/4 miles round trip.

TERRAIN: Steep mountain near the coast, covered with alternating brush and forest.

ELEVATION GAIN/LOSS: 750 feet+/750 feet−

BEST TIME: Spring. Fall and summer are good, too.

WARNINGS: No water along trail. Nearest year-round facilities at Whitethorn, Redway. Timber rattlers live in this area.

DIRECTIONS TO TRAILHEAD: Leave Highway 101 at Garberville on the south or at Redway on the north. Take Briceland Road from Redway (2.8 miles north of Garberville on Business 101). In 12 1/2 miles, take the left fork to Whitethorn. In 4 1/2 more miles come to the junction known as Four Corners. (The unmarked Usal Road is on the left, straight ahead is the Sinkyone.) Turn right and go 2 miles on a winding dirt road to Wailaki Campground. Trail leaves from south end of campground. (If you are riding horses it is better to leave from Nadelos Camp, 1/2 mile farther.)

FURTHER INFO: Bureau of Land Management (707) 462-3873.

Beyond them however, looking out over the landscape, you have to conclude that there is not much settlement in these parts. To the south at least 14 different coastal ridges can be spotted on a clear day. Immediately to the south Chemise Mountain drops off into the deep canyon of Whale Gulch, the Sinkyone Wilderness and precipitous Anderson Cliffs just beyond. South of there are Cape Vizcaino, Kibesillah Hill, Ten Mile river mouth and dunes, the Georgia-Pacific smokestack in Fort Bragg and Sherwood Ridge extending inland from there. Greenwood

Ridge forms the horizon on the south. To your east all of the Yolla Bollies rise to their 7000-foot summits. On the north may be seen Shelter Cove and the 4087-foot hulk of Kings Peak.

Leading south from the summit you can follow an old pack trail along the ridge. In less than 1/4 mile you will come to the secondary peak of Chemise Flat. Though not as high in elevation, this peak is more open on top, providing better views directly south into the Sinkyone. A small dry camp is perched on this summit. Beyond here, however, the trail south along the ridge becomes ever more choked with brush. Some day this will become a portion of a continuous trail planned to traverse the entire Lost Coast, from the Mattole River on the north to Usal Creek on the south, about 55 miles. For now, the overgrown trail does continue to Whale Gulch, but it is not recommended. It is a bushwacker's delight. Return on the same trail you ascended.

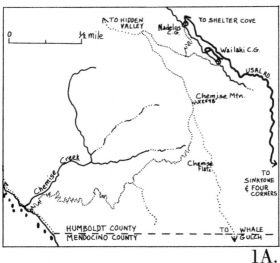

1A.

CHEMISE MOUNTAIN to BEACH
STEEP TRAIL TO A SECRET BEACH

The trail is NOT RECOMMENDED, EXCEPT *for the hardy and well prepared. It has been included because it provides the only access to a rugged 2-mile stretch of wilderness beach.*

From the summit, follow a broad firebreak 250 feet

CHEMISE MOUNTAIN to BEACH:

DISTANCE: 9 miles round trip to beach (includes the 2 3/4 miles of above hike).

TERRAIN: Extremely steep switchbacking trail through brushy forest to an isolated beach. Last 200 precipitous feet assisted by ropes anchored to the cliff.

ELEVATION GAIN/LOSS: Over 3000 feet each way. Unforgettable climb out.

BEST TIME: Spring, summer, fall.

WARNINGS: Most difficult trail in this book! No water along trail. Carry plenty. Only endurance hikers or runners should attempt this in a day. Last part of trail to beach is steep and treacherous. Go with a friend. Inquire at Bureau of Land Management before going. Trail is often impassable due to slides.

DIRECTIONS TO TRAILHEAD: Same as #1.

FURTHER INFO: Bureau of Land Management (707) 462-3873.

to another sign indicating the trail to the beach. Here you can look down a firebreak along a steeply descending ridge. In a major fire in 1973, this break saved the pristine area to the south. The trail wanders in and out of the fire area as it descends to the beach. For the first 1/4 mile you descend steeply, entering a stand of knobcone pine, a tree that requires fire for its seeds to sprout.

For the next 1/4 mile, your descent eases somewhat, wandering through dense hardwood forest and a couple of dry gullies. At 5/8 mile from the summit, you can hear Chemise Creek below you. (It is a long way down to water though.) This is a pleasant, shady portion of the hike. At 3/4 mile you have gained the ridge just south of Chemise Creek. The trail heads west and down the ridge.

Soon a sign indicates that you are one mile from the summit and that it is 2 miles farther to the beach. Nearby the hardwood forest opens up to provide the first views since the summit. A little farther you

reach another firebreak. A spur trail leads south, dead ending in 3/4 mile. The beach trail winds down the firebreak here, soon reaching a flat where you might camp. The trail continues down the firebreak, then plunges down a steep hill to the north of the break. Here you quickly encounter Sitka spruce, including two forked giants charred but not killed by the fire.

At a small meadow just beyond the 2-mile point, you come to the last level ground before the beach. This meadow, at 1200 feet, is a fine place to camp if you do not want to carry your pack down to the beach and back.

At the edge of the meadow you get one more warning: a charred sign indicates "DANGER — STEEP TRAIL." A clearing provides a glimpse of the ocean far below you in case you still had doubts. From here the extremely steep trail descends by numerous switchbacks to the anchored ropes which provide welcome hand holds on the last plunge to the beach.

Just in case you had any thoughts of walking out of here in a different way than you came, the beach is impassable to the south within a mile or so of the trail at a rocky outcrop known as Point No Pass. A second Point No Pass one mile north of the trail can be walked around only during minus tides of −1.0 or lower. From there you can walk the beach north to Shelter Cove. Be sure you leave sufficient time to get around the rocky point at low tide. This exit may involve some rock scrambling. Otherwise be sure you have enough time for your arduous climb up the mountain. Take plenty of water.

SINKYONE WILDERNESS STATE PARK:

GENERAL DIRECTIONS: Leave Highway 101, at Garberville if you are coming from the south, or at Redway from the north. Take Briceland Road west from Redway (2.8 miles north of Garberville on the old highway). In 12 miles take the left fork to Whitethorn (the last outpost of civilization — the sign says Coors). Just 4 1/2 miles beyond the store you come to the junction known as Four Corners.

On the left is the Usal Road, to the right leads to King Range Conservation Area. Go straight ahead to the main part of the Sinkyone, 3.6 miles farther to the visitor center, down a steep, winding dirt road (not advisable to campers, RV's or motor homes at any time, may be impassable in rainy months to most vehicles).

The Sinkyone may also be reached in good weather over the rough but spectacular Usal Road. This is a county maintained road, but only during the summer months, generally May-September. It is 24 miles from where Usal Road leaves Highway 1 at M.90.88 to Four Corners. The road gets rougher at the north end.

FURTHER INFO: Sinkyone Wilderness State Park (707) 946-2311, 247-3318.

ENVIRONMENTAL CAMPS: There are 7 walk-in camps in the park. Six are down the hill, the other is Low Gap environmental camp. From Four Corners, go south up a steep winding grade for 2.3 miles, where the trail to the camp is on the left. It is 1/10 mile walk into the five campsites, located on a gentle stream in a redwood grove. This camp may be a sunny, warm retreat, if the fog has moved in to shroud the coast in gray dampness. Across the road from Low Gap Camp is the top end of the Low Gap trail, a 1 1/2 mile shuttle which drops 900 feet to join the park road near the visitor center.

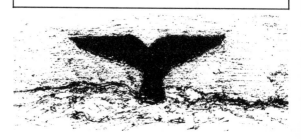

SINKYONE WILDERNESS STATE PARK

INCLUDES THE NEXT FIVE TRAILS

Located in the extreme northwestern corner of Mendocino County, the Sinkyone (sing-key-own) preserves a sample of the rugged wilderness that once existed all along the Mendocino Coast. Though the Sinkyone was settled in the 1860s, and was logged and ranched for much of the next century, it now stands as a largely pristine wilderness. The State Park was established in 1976.

The Sinkyone contains numerous interwoven environments within its 3576 acres: black sand beaches, tide pools, coastal cliffs, lush coastal streams, grassy headlands, old homestead and town sites, untouched virgin forests, logged-over areas, and high ridges. All of these can be reached on one or more of the trails which follow.

The Sinkyone Wilderness State Park is unlike any other park in the State system. It can be reached only by isolated, unpaved mountain roads which are often impassable in winter. There are no campgrounds where you can park next to your campsite; you must hike at least 200 feet to camp. There is no entrance station nor day-use fee. The visitor center is located in a rustic old ranch house with no electricity or telephone. The nearest gas station and store are far from the park boundary. While rangers do patrol the park regularly, do not expect to find one at a moment's notice, or even see one every day.

If this scenario does not appeal to you, you would do best not to visit the Sinkyone. While you can visit the park as a long day trip, you will enjoy it far more if you can stay overnight, or even better, a week.

The Sinkyone was named for the Indian tribe which originally inhabited this rugged country. They were the southernmost of the Athabascan language tribes on the coast. Known for their backwoods skills, the Sinkyone tribe was small and disorganized. They were quickly overrun by the whites who came to find land.

On the brighter side, a four-legged group of Sinkyone natives have recently been relocated in the park. At last count there were 19 Roosevelt elk located within park boundaries. These large animals stand five feet at the shoulder. The males grow up to 1100 pounds, with antlers up to six feet, which they shed in fall.

The elk originally inhabited all of the Mendocino Coast, but were hunted nearly to extinction. A large herd has lived many years at Prairie Creek Redwoods State Park in Humboldt County, from where these elk were relocated. They are easily approached. But if you run from a bull, he will give chase, running up to 35 mph. Don't let one chase you up a tree, especially in rut season in September.

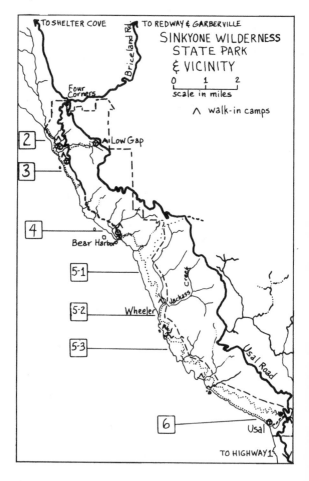

WHALE GULCH:

DISTANCE: 2 miles round trip.
TERRAIN: Deep, verdant coastal stream canyon running parallel to the coast, including two coastal lakes at an elevation of 100 feet.
ELEVATION GAIN/LOSS: 300 feet+/300 feet−
BEST TIME: Spring. Summer is OK. Rather dry by fall.
WARNINGS: Be prepared for a steep hill on the hike out. Stinging nettles and poison oak abound. Isolated country with no services.
DIRECTIONS TO TRAILHEAD: Follow general directions to Sinkyone State Park. The trail leaves Sinkyone Road 2.3 miles from Four Corners, or 1.3 miles north of visitor center. Sign at trailhead indicates trail to Jones Beach Environmental Camp (no mention of Whale Gulch). Jones Beach Environmental Camp is 1/6 mile down a steep grade by a stream beneath a eucalyptus grove. When you park your car, make sure it is securely situated on this steep roadside (block the wheels!).
FURTHER INFO: Sinkyone Wilderness State Park (707) 986-7711 or (707) 946-2311.

2.

WHALE GULCH
COASTAL STREAM AND LAKE HABITAT

Your trail follows an old road down a steep hill for the first 1/8 mile. Your descent eases as the trail curves to the right, approaching a grove of large eucalyptus. Nestled in these trees is the first of the Jones Beach campsites. In 50 feet you meet an old road which runs north-south across the bluffs. Go right.

About 1/4 mile from the trailhead you cross a small creek. An old car was long ago used as fill at this creek crossing. You can see it in the creek bed on the left, with a tree growing through it. Two more camps are just beyond, one of them under beautiful trees with calla lilies growing nearby.

The trail forks shortly, the left fork heading down to the beach. Take the right fork to Whale Gulch. In about 1/8 mile you can look down the deep gully of an unnamed creek to Jones Beach. Then your trail draws progressively closer to the deep canyon. Perhaps this was once a tidal estuary before geological forces uplifted this old marine terrace to its present level.

At 7/16 mile from the trailhead your trail crosses a tributary stream. Just to your left the creek plunges into the deep verdant canyon. You may glimpse the ocean over the razor ridge to the west. Sounds of creek and waterfall mingle with the crashing of the surf.

At 1/2 mile you are again along the edge of the canyon. From here the trail gradually descends into the canyon. The next section can be very marshy, especially in spring. You cross the main creek. At 9/16 mile you ford a small tributary and come to the first of two lakes. Iris grow along the shore. Cattails grow in the shallows. If the stream was in fact a tidal estuary in eons past, then these lakes were saltwater tidal lagoons.

The trail continues to the right of the lake, climbing to higher and drier ground. The 3/4 mile point places you between the two lakes. You can see high cliffs ahead to your northwest. To continue, go uphill to the right of a stand of alders. At 7/8 mile the ocean comes into view to the northwest. You are at the top of the upper lake. Go 1/16 mile farther and you are overlooking deep, rugged Whale Gulch. Driftwood logs are jammed into a small lagoon at the mouth of Whale Gulch Creek. To the right is the creek's steep canyon and a waterfall.

Though the trail continues steeply down into the gulch, it is on private property. To continue requires the owner's permission.* Retrace your steps back along the canyon and up the steep hill to your car.

---

* Eventually the state hopes to acquire the Whale Gulch property. This is planned to be a portion of the continuous Lost Coast trail.

NEEDLE ROCK to FLAT ROCK CREEK:

DISTANCE: 1 1/2 miles one-way, 3 miles round trip.
TERRAIN: Grassy headlands, stairway to a long broad, dark sand beach.
ELEVATION GAIN/LOSS: 190 feet+/190 feet−
BEST TIME: Medium to low tide.
WARNINGS: Never turn your back on the ocean; rogue waves can strike any time, especially in winter.
DIRECTIONS TO TRAILHEAD: From Sinkyone Park visitor center, trail leads west.
FURTHER INFO: Sinkyone Wilderness State Park (707) 946-2311.
ENVIRONMENTAL CAMPS: A separate trail starts east of the barn (north of the visitor center) leading to Needle Rock Environmental Camp. There are two campsites and a toilet within 200 feet of the barn. Streamside Environmental Camp is 1/4 mile north along the same trail (or it can be reached by walking southwest from the Low Gap Trailhead). It consists of two camps in a protected riparian glen and a third camp on a nearby knoll with a panoramic ocean view.

3.

NEEDLE ROCK
to FLAT ROCK CREEK

LONG, DARK SAND BEACH

The trail starts directly across the road from the visitor center. Go west over gently sloping, grassy headlands past a giant cypress snag. Just over 1/16 mile you come to a long winding stairway which takes you to the beach just east of Double Rock. Needle Rock is visible not far to the north. (You may also walk north along the beach past Needle Rock to Jones Beach, 3/4 mile north, where another stairway leads up to headlands.)

Your walk heads south along the dark sand beach, beside high cliffs. The cliffs are cut by several steep gulches which may have waterfalls in spring. The deepest gulch, about halfway to the end of the beach, generally has a stream throughout the year. South of there, the beach widens. The cliffs are cut by even more steep gulches. Near its south end the beach becomes very broad, then comes to a point. Directly off the point are several flat tidal rocks which you can climb onto at medium to low tide. There are small tide pools here.

Just southeast of the point, where the beach narrows and comes to a creek, is a stairway. This leads up to the bluffs to a path ending at the main road just north of the rough crossing at Flat Rock Creek. Or you may walk back the way you came.

4.

BEAR HARBOR
FROM ROAD'S END TO AN OLD HOMESTEAD

The Bear Harbor trail crosses Orchard Creek on a small wooden footbridge. The nearly level trail follows along the creek through lush riparian vegetation. At 1/8 mile you enter a grove of tall eucalyptus trees, quickly coming upon the path to Railroad Creek Camp on the left. Just beyond the low brushy ridge on your right lies a narrow beach.

Railroad Creek acquired its name in the early days of logging. The railroad ran up this creek to the

BEAR HARBOR:

DISTANCE: 3/4 mile to 3 3/4 miles round trip, depending on road conditions.

TERRAIN: Verdant, coastal stream canyon, leading to a secluded beach.

BEST TIME: Spring is best. Summer, fall OK.

WARNINGS: Stinging nettles and poison oak grow in profusion along sections of the trail. Isolated country with no services. If not camping, leave ample time before dark to walk back to your car.

DIRECTIONS TO TRAILHEAD: Follow general directions to Sinkyone State Park. One mile beyond the visitor center a sign says "No vehicles advised beyond this point." The main problem lies in a deep gully 1/2 mile beyond the sign at the Flat Rock Creek crossing. Generally a four-wheel-drive or any high-clearance vehicle can easily cross this gully, except perhaps at high water. Some passenger cars have even gone beyond. If you have doubts, consult with the ranger. *Do not take chances: no tow truck is around to pull you out.* Walk or drive to where the road is blocked by a fence near Orchard Creek. Bear Harbor is just 3/8 mile beyond.

FURTHER INFO: Sinkyone Wilderness State Park (707) 946-2311.

ENVIRONMENTAL CAMPS: Orchard Creek Camp is 200 feet upstream (to the northeast) at the end of the road, by a pioneer apple orchard. Railroad Creek Camp is 1/8 mile down the trail from the end of the road, in a eucalyptus grove planted by pioneers. Bear Harbor Camp is in a meadow surrounding an old homestead site, just a stone's throw from the beach of Bear Harbor.

area where many big redwoods were felled. The bucked-up logs were loaded onto the short line railroad and hauled to Bear Harbor to be loaded onto the lumber schooners that called there. As you cross another footbridge across Railroad Creek, your trail follows the old railroad bed for most of the next 1/4 mile to Bear Harbor. Just before you reach the campground at the site of Bear Harbor Ranch, the railroad bed veers to the right across the creek and starts to climb the overgrown ridge to the location of the loading chute at the tip of the point. Iron rails can still be seen protruding from the cliff there.

The sandy cove of Bear Harbor lies just beyond the old house site. Near a corral to the east is the start of the new Bear Harbor to Usal trail (see trail #5). Scattered near the junction of the two creeks are many domesticated plants gone wild from the old ranch garden: calla lilies, narcissus, yellow water iris, blue creeping myrtle, Port Orford cedar, pampas grass and an old holly bush. The creek has been diverted around the old home site by a stone wall. Notice how well the old ranch house was situated to give it maximum protection from the strong winds which blow here most of the time. Along the tideline on the nearby beach can be found bits of brick and pottery from the old ranch.

You can walk about 1/4 mile south along the dark sand beach. Sea birds nest in the cliffs above and in the sea stacks offshore. The large sea stack directly offshore is Cluster Cone Rock. As you walk along the beach, keep an ear cocked for the sound of landslides from the precipitous slopes above you. You can see evidence of several slides, most prominently the old one which blocks passage to the jagged point at the south end of the beach, consisting of rocks up to the size of houses. This area is continually subject to some powerful forces of nature. When the author first visited Bear Harbor in 1976, the hull of a wrecked boat was wedged in the rocks at high tide line. Ten years later nothing remains.

As you return along the beach, keep an eye on the rocky promontory where the loading chute once was. Hawks and ravens frequent this perch, perusing the area for food or intruders. At low tide you can walk west across the driftwood at the mouth of the creek and out to the point. It is an easy scramble over the rocks to the otherwise inaccessible beach west of the ridge. *Just be very careful that the rising tide does not trap you on the wrong side of the point.* To the north-west lies Morgan Rock, bleached white with guano. Notice its flat top; another loading pier, known as Bear Landing, once reached out to this rock.

It is a short, easy walk back to your car if you were able to drive to the end of the road. Leave extra time however, if you had to park 1 1/2 miles farther up the road.

5.

NEW LOST COAST
RUGGED NEW BACKPACK ROUTE

The New Lost Coast Trail traverses the most spectacu-lar portion of the Mendocino Coast, rugged, isolated country which was never tamed by civilization. Thomas Merton, famed religious writer and world traveler, considered it one of the most beautiful places in the world. Upon visiting in 1967 he said of the virgin forests of the Sinkyone (then known as Bear Harbor) "Who can bear to see such trees and be away from them."

This trail was just being completed at publication time. Trail construction crews worked overtime to fin-ish it before the end of 1986. This trail report covers the first 4 1/2 miles in detail, then summarizes the rest of the route.

You must have a topo map and compass (and the ability to use them) to safely walk the trail. Even then, the trail is not marked on the topo map; if you stray off the trail, it can be difficult to relocate. If you decide to take the trail south of Wheeler, travel with a friend. Make sure another friend knows where you have gone and when you should return.

5-1.

NEW LOST COAST
BEAR HARBOR TO WHEELER

Go east from Bear Harbor, passing the corral and trail register. In 1/4 mile you cross a tiny bridge. Here the grassy canyon becomes more wooded as the

NEW LOST COAST:

DISTANCE: 16 1/2 miles one-way.

TERRAIN: Rugged coastal canyons and ridges.

ELEVATION GAIN/LOSS: Bear Harbor to Wheeler 1200 feet+/1200 feet−. For the rest of trail: estimated at 5000 feet+/5000 feet−, or more.

BEST TIME: Spring. Summer and fall are next best.

WARNINGS: Isolated country far from towns and traveled roads. Hike with a companion. Requires map and compass and the ability to use them. Timber rattlesnakes, scorpions, ticks, poison oak and stinging nettles all occur along the trail. Watch out and keep away from them. Beyond Wheeler (at 4 1/2 miles) this route is one of the most arduous in this book. You must have a permit to hike this trail. This is the perfect time to inquire about trail conditions/completion status. Camping is allowed only in designated areas.

DIRECTIONS TO TRAILHEAD: Follow general directions to Sinkyone State Park, then proceed to Bear Harbor. (If you cannot drive beyond Flat Rock Creek, add 1.5 miles to total distance.) The trail is marked "Lost Coast Trail" at the corral near Bear Harbor Environmental Camp, just east of the camp.

FEES: Permit required. $1 per person per day.

FURTHER INFO: Sinkyone Wilderness State Park (707) 946-2311.

trail starts to climb. That pungent smell comes from the bay laurel trees which surround you. Other plants found here include red alders, big leaf maples, elderberries and many ferns. Just beyond 3/8 mile you cross the creek. Tank up on water here. It is 1 1/2 miles to the next stream.

The trail switchbacks to the right and climbs steadily out of the canyon. At 1/2 mile a grassy clearing gives you a view up the canyon to heavily wooded ridges.

As you gain the ridge the flora changes: huckleberry, wild rose and iris grow beside the trail. At 3/4 mile you are on the first of many old logging roads which the trail follows. Your "skid trail" soon tops the crest of the ridge, where you get glimpses up and down the spectacular coast.

At one mile the trail switches away from one logging road, then promptly joins another. You see your first redwoods by the trail here. Nearby grow orchid-like slink pod (fetid adder's tongue) plants with shiny spotted leaves.

At 1 3/16 miles your trail tops the next ridge, providing a great view of Bear Harbor and Cluster Cone Rocks below. After a fairly level stretch, the trail plunges steeply into Duffys Gulch.

Here the trail leaves the logging road and joins a portion of the original Humboldt Trail, built in 1862 when the entire coast was opened to homesteading. Remarkably the trail bed has withstood 124 years of wet coastal winters and 54 years of disuse. A Pomo Indian was the last person known to traverse the old trail. He rode a horse from Usal to Shelter Cove in 1922.

The trail descends eastward into Duffys Gulch as you begin to spot virgin redwoods. There are no stumps in the canyon. As you descend more steeply, the gurgling of the stream can be heard over the roaring of the surf. As the trail switchbacks down to the creek crossing, thousand-year-old redwoods to 10 feet in diameter grow beside grand fir, Douglas fir and bay laurel. Look up to your left at a towering rock overhang; a large fir tree grows atop the rock. Over the creek crossing grows a giant big leaf maple with a crown 80 feet across.

Take a minute to quench your thirst and fill your canteen, a great opportunity to marvel at the virgin beauty of this place. Along the creek below the giant redwoods grow five-finger, woodwardia, sword and common lady ferns. Nearby grow Pacific waterleaf (with odd green flowers), redwood sorrel, pig-a-back plant, huckleberry, Douglas iris and an occasional leather fern and calypso orchid. Poison oak is also common here, so watch for it, especially along the densely grown section of trail which follows. You have come 1 3/4 miles from Bear Harbor.

You then climb out of the gulch by a recently reworked but still uneven section of trail. Large tree roots have overgrown the trail; watch your step. Below and to the west through the trees you can glimpse

the rugged mouth of this steep gulch. As the trail levels, alder and tanoak replace laurel and maple as the deciduous trees.

Nearly 2 1/2 miles from the trailhead, you leave the forest for steep, open coastal grasslands. The next section traverses the grassy bluffs through a series of small gullies and rises. Indian paintbrush, buttercups, blue-eyed grass, lupine, dandelion and golden poppies add color as the sound of the pounding surf rises from below. Expansive views of the Sinkyone lie to the north. Near a small sign indicating the halfway point to Wheeler grows a large ceanothus in tree form. Over 20 feet tall, its fragrant blue blossoms litter the trail in spring.

At 2 3/8 miles you plunge into the first of several dark forests along the ridge which you follow to Wheeler. After another stretch of grasslands, you enter another fir forest, this one almost flat and very rocky. Just beyond on the left is a sinkhole or slough pocket, a natural drainage with no above ground outlet. This formed as coastal uplifting occurred to the west of the drainage, causing it to find an underground outlet. As your trail follows along the western edge of the sinkhole, notice the dense vegetation in its protected microclimate.

At 2 1/2 miles the trail passes through dense brush, then uphill with the sinkhole still on your left. After passing a gnarled, wind-topped old redwood, you come to more grasslands. At 2 3/4 miles you again enter forest, quickly coming to a nice stand of redwoods.

Your trail then switchbacks to the left and up a small draw. As you come to the ridge, you meet a small side trail. This overgrown old trail climbs the ridge northeast to connect with Usal Road near the site of the old town of Kenny. Though the trail is marked intermittently with orange, white and blue plastic flagging, it is hard bushwhacking through rugged country. The trail is not recommended. (It is hoped that State Parks will reopen this trail after they finish the new Lost Coast Trail.)

The main trail climbs steeply southeast up the narrow ridge to its top. Along this stretch grow trillium, iris, redwood sorrel, one-leaved wild onion, slink pod, miners lettuce and columbine. At the top, about 3 miles from the trailhead, you parallel an old fence before descending steeply to the east, then the south. You then climb steeply again to another top, then drop again by switchbacks before climbing to a third top near 3 1/4 miles. From here you can look east into the heavily wooded drainage of Jackass Creek.

Then you descend more gradually along the east side of the ridge through mixed conifer forest before you switch sharply right and downhill through bluffs of low brush and grass. This open section of trail has many foxgloves, ceanothus, tall brodiaeas, blue-eyed grass, sticky monkeyflowers and beach strawberries, not to mention poison oak.

At 3 1/2 miles you are in grasslands following the edge of the forest. You soon approach a gnarled old redwood grove, the trees windswept and stunted, but surviving. Behind their dense vegetation lies another slough pocket. Two narrow paths into the depression are guarded by poison oak and easily missed. If you find your way, however, you enter a protected small virgin redwood grove, a little refuge where the silence of the trees overcomes the roar of surf and wind outside. Two old fire rings lie in the grove, but FIRES ARE NOT ALLOWED HERE.

At nearly 3 3/4 miles from Bear Harbor, your trail turns northeast away from the coast and the ridge you have been following. Coming to a clearing as you descend into a canyon, you can see the old Wheeler road in a flat grassy opening 600 feet below; you will be there soon. The trail drops rapidly now by a series of long switchbacks.

You soon come to two large, gnarled old-growth redwoods, surrounded by smaller redwoods, then descend into a fern-filled gulch by two more switchbacks, coming to big redwoods and ferns at the bottom of the canyon. On your left you will pass the famed toilet tree. In another 100 feet you come to a flat grassy opening beside Jackass Creek. Nearby is a campsite beneath two large redwoods. This is Jackass Creek, also known as Wolf Creek, also known as Wheeler.

If you need to hike out the same day, be sure to leave three hours of daylight to get you back to your car or camp.

5-2.

NEW LOST COAST
GHOST TOWN OF WHEELER

As you come to the flat along the North Fork of Jackass Creek, the main campsite lies just ahead. A second campsite is 200 feet south, near the creek crossing. From the second camp, the foundation of the old school building is on your right. (This is called Schoolmarm Grove.) Fifty feet uphill from the foundation is a plastic pipe which comes from a spring. This water source was safe in May 1986; best to use this as a dozen cattle still graze Wheeler.

Most of the town of Wheeler was to the south of the school. Wheeler was established in 1950, one of the last logging company towns, and probably the newest ghost town in the West. The town lasted for only 10 years. Established by the Wheeler family as the Wolf Creek Timber Co. (you wouldn't call it Jackass Timber, would you?), the town housed about 32 families who harvested the timber, worked in the state-of-the-art sawmill, and hauled the cut lumber by truck to Willits. The modern town had electricity, telephones and a water system.

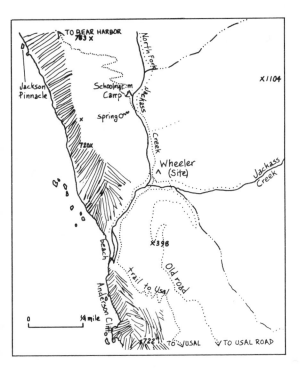

The trail into "town" crosses the creek over a large log, remnant of an old bridge. Across the creek, the trail heads south on the old road. It passes more foundations, a few logging relics and a side street or two. Domesticated plants grow wild in the lush habitat: foxglove, spearmint, red hot poker and alyssum. About 1/4 mile from the creek crossing you come to the heart of town. The sawmill was located here at the confluence of the North Fork and the main fork of the creek.

The trail crosses the creek, heading generally south, coming to the beach in another 1/8 mile. The narrow, dark sand beach is guarded by high cliffs on either side. It is backed by a small lagoon and a large grassy flat where silverweed grows. Harbor seals and sea birds frequent the beach.

The trail south heads up the grassy gulch to the southeast. This was where the bosses lived. With its spectacular view of the beach, it is easily the most beautiful site, though not the most protected. About 5/8 mile south of Schoolmarm Grove you come to a beautiful wildflower garden at the end of the cleared portion of the gulch. As the small creek forks just up canyon, the newly worked trail plunges into the

39

dense growth, climbing steeply. (See next report for a summary of the trail south.)

You may loop back to camp on the main road, crossing the creek about 1/8 mile east of the confluence. By the way, locals call it Wolf Creek because the wind sometimes sounds like howling wolves as it rushes through the canyon.

5-3.

NEW LOST COAST

WHEELER TO USAL

The trail south is spectacular but very steep and difficult. If you head toward Usal, be sure to have a full canteen, topo map and compass. Make sure a friend knows where you are and when you plan to return. The rough terrain restricts most backpackers to a pace of about one mile per hour. Though it is just 12 miles to Usal, two nights stopover are recommended.

You leave the beach and the bosses' gulch, climbing steeply through dense brush, then into tall forest. You soon come to an 800-foot-high ridge, which you contour south before dropping steeply into the deep gulch of Little Jackass Creek. At the bottom, you come to old corrals, all that remain of a pre-1900 logging town. Nearby is another environmental camp.

Another arduous climb takes you out of Little Jackass and over another high ridge. You then descend into Northport Gulch, site of another pre-1900 logging camp.

This pattern continues through rugged, spectacular country for another 8 miles. Climb steeply to another ridge, then plunge into Anderson Gulch. Here another camp sits above the stream, overlooking the mouth of the brushy gulch. It is 5 miles from this last camp to the trailhead at Usal.

A shorter climb leads to steep, grassy headlands which you contour above the shore. Then a short descent brings you to fern-filled Dark Gulch.

Now you make one last long ascent, climbing 1200 feet in 1 1/4 miles to just below the 1320-foot summit of Timber Point. The last 2 5/8 miles of trail meanders along the ridge before dropping by switchbacks to meet Usal Road, 6.14 miles north of Highway 1.

USAL WATERFALL:

DISTANCE: 4 1/2 miles round trip.

TERRAIN: Rocky beach at the foot of steep cliffs.

BEST TIME: Spring. By summer the falls are just a trickle. Extreme low tide is best, though passable at moderate low tide.

WARNINGS: Not passable at medium to high tide. Always watch the ocean for oversize rogue waves. Isolated country. Nearest services: south at Westport and east at Leggett. The only water is from local creeks, which dry up in summer. Road may be impassable in rainy season. Due to steep curves, it is never passable to RV's or trailers. Use of motorbikes off road prohibited.

DIRECTIONS TO TRAILHEAD: Turn west off Highway 1 at M.90.88 (road on left when going north) onto unpaved, unmarked Usal Road. The road quickly climbs to 1000 feet, providing spectacular coastal views. It then descends by abrupt, steep switchbacks to the flat near the mouth of Usal Creek. Cross a narrow wooden bridge over the creek into Usal campground. Then turn left at M.6.00 onto the rough, short road to the beach.

FURTHER INFO: Sinkyone Wilderness State Park. (707) 946-2311.

OTHER SUGGESTION: NEW LOST COAST TRAIL, SOUTH END: The trail has been reconstructed on the south end. It leaves the Usal Road at M.6.14, climbing quickly to spectacular views of the beach and Usal Creek.

6.

USAL WATERFALL
SOUTH END OF THE SINKYONE

Usal Beach and the adjacent steep bluffs were the southern end of the Sinkyone Indians' territory. The Sinkyone name for the place was Djokniki. The name Usal (Youshal on early maps) is believed to have originated in the Pomo words for southeast.

After 1867, Usal saw a number of white travelers since it was on the Humboldt Trail, which led along the coast from Fort Bragg to Eureka. But the first white settlers did not come to Usal to stay until 1889. Then 50 to 100 men came to install a lumber mill and loading wharf for the Usal Redwood Co. Usal had some of the largest trees in Mendocino County, untouched until then. The large mill was built and in operation by 1892, along with a 1600-foot-long wharf (!) and 3 miles of railroad up the creek.

In 1894 Robert Dollar bought the whole operation. It is claimed that Dollar was able to purchase it because he owned the steamship Newsboy and was able to land where other ships refused to call, Usal being the most dangerous of all the doghole ports. The mill shut down in 1900. This was largely because the huge trees were inferior to (though probably older than) those used for lumber elsewhere on the coast, yielding only half the lumber that its size indicated. In 1902 the idle mill burned down, along with most of the town.

Robert Dollar went on to build his fortune with the Dollar Steamship Line, later President Lines. Usal became one of the first of many logging ghost towns along the Mendocino Coast.

Usal Beach has seen many years of public use. Without supervision, some visitors to Usal developed bad habits: littering, shooting up signs and tearing about indiscriminately on motor bikes. The wilderness at Usal suffered: the place started looking torn up, public safety could not be guaranteed.

Georgia-Pacific Corp. finally decided that if they could not control the situation (which they could not), that it would be better to lease the land to the State Park System. The lease is now in effect and slowly things are starting to change at Usal.

The first step was to ban off-road vehicles from the heavily eroded hill climbs above the beach. Now vehicles are confined to designated roads and the beach area at Usal, with a speed limit of 15 MPH in the camp (25 MPH on the beach). Riders of off-road vehicles are also warned that unlicensed vehicles and drivers operating on a county road (the Usal Road) are in violation of both Park and State Vehicle Code Sections. These regulations are being enforced by the State Park rangers. A ranger outpost is expected to be established at Usal in summer 1986.

Hunting or shooting are no longer permitted in the camp area. Dogs must be leashed and licensed here just like other State Park lands. Fires are permitted only in the fire rings which have been installed. All refuse must be packed out, as there are no trash receptacles. As soon as camping facilities are completed, there will be a $3 per night fee, with an additional $3 per extra vehicle and $1 per dog.

It is hoped that these improvements will help to stem the careless degradation of this otherwise pristine area. Please cooperate, and report violations to the Sinkyone rangers. The wilderness heals itself, but only if we treat it with love and respect.

Have you checked your tide table? Make sure you are interpreting current tide information correctly, as the cliffs behind this narrow beach are unforgiving. It is best to start this hike two hours or more *before* low tide.

This beach hike starts where the beach road ends, just north of the mouth of Usal Creek. You walk northwest along the dark sand and gravel beach, at the base of 400-foot cliffs. Large rocks lie scattered along the beach, mostly at the base of the slide-torn cliffs.

You may share the beach with off-road vehicles, but within a mile large boulders prevent vehicles from passing. The cliffs on your right become even higher as you walk toward the waterfall, which can be seen falling to the beach near the point. Approximately 1 1/4 miles, 1320-foot-high Timber Point lies hidden above you at the top of the cliffs, less than a half mile away. This is more than a 100% slope (a 45° angle). Also near this point, two small seasonal streams cascade down to the beach. They are not dependable as a water source, drying up by summer.

You continue northwest on the narrowing beach, which is more rocky than sandy for the rest of the hike. A few small sea stacks lie offshore. Several rock outcrops along this stretch would bar passage if it were not low tide.

After 2 miles, the waterfall, if it is flowing, pulls at your attention. When it is in full force, billows of spray fly in all directions. As you walk around one more rocky outcrop, the falls are not far ahead.

At 2 1/4 miles you come to the falls. Here the beach ends, as the waterfall tumbles onto rocks just short of the point. It takes a minus tide of −1.5 or lower to be able to walk around the point. *Even then be sure you do not get trapped on the wrong side of the point by the rising tide*. It would be a long, rugged bushwhack up Dark Gulch to join the New Lost Coast trail and follow that back to Usal.

As you walk back along the beach, there are spectacular views south along the coast to the jagged point of Cape Vizcaino and the rest of the Mendocino Coast beyond.

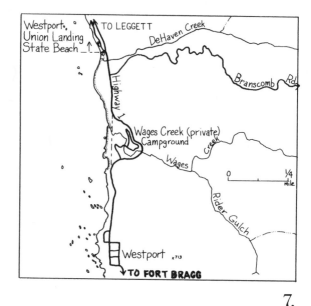

7.

DeHAVEN CREEK to WAGES CREEK
SANDY BEACH ALONG THE ROCKY SHORE

The trail starts 100 feet south of the parking lot. A sign indicates no motor vehicles beyond the trailhead. The trail drops quickly to a rocky beach. You soon come to a ford of DeHaven Creek. It is an easy ford in summer, but in winter you may get wet feet.

Just over 1/8 mile from the trailhead, you come to a rocky point. Here you must gauge if the tide is low enough to continue. If the tide is rising and the water is coming over the tidal rocks onto the beach, *do not go*.

The beach widens just around this point. Rocky

DeHAVEN CREEK to WAGES CREEK:

DISTANCE: 1 1/2 to 2 1/2 miles round trip.

TERRAIN: Sandy beach.

BEST TIME: Medium to low tide.

WARNINGS: Impassable at high tide. Always watch the ocean for killer waves. Private property at south end. Stay on sand. Also private property on bluffs to east.

DIRECTIONS TO TRAILHEAD: Turn west off Highway 1 at M.79.3, north of Westport. Parking lot is 150 feet north of entrance.

FURTHER INFO: Mendocino Area State Parks (707) 937-5804.

OTHER SUGGESTION: The blufftop from this trailhead north to Howard Creek is traversed by a paved road 1 1/5 miles long. Though open to motor traffic (campground access), it is a good place to explore on bicycles, on foot or in a wheelchair. Watch out for traffic as you follow the rugged, rocky shoreline.

tidepools are on your right, blanketed with seaweed and very slippery. At 1/4 mile you come around a second rocky point. The view opens up to the south; you can see Wages Creek beach 1/2 mile ahead, the buildings of Westport visible beyond.

The beach widens again near 3/8 mile. The rocky tidepools on the right give way to scattered small rocks. The cliffs to the left are lower here.

A little beyond 1/2 mile the cliffs end. You come to a very wide beach at the broad canyon of Wages Creek. A private campground is up in the canyon — KEEP OUT! At 3/4 mile you come to Wages Creek, running along the cliff at the south end of the beach. At this point you must decide whether to return for a 1 1/2 mile round trip or continue, if the tide is still low enough.

If you decide to continue, it is easiest to ford the creek about 100 feet upstream from its mouth. You soon come to a sea stack on your right at the edge of the beach. You can walk into its wave tunnel at low tide to examine the tidal creatures. Goose neck and volcano-shaped barnacles, limpets and a few mussels grow on the east side. The seaward side has more mussels and some anemones.

Beyond the sea stack, the narrow sand strip broadens to another beach. This ends 1/8 mile beyond at yet another rocky point. To continue you must scramble over rocks for 150 feet. (Again, make sure the tide is low enough!) Then another long beach extends for 1/8 mile to more rocks. You are now 1 1/4 miles from your car. If you walk out on the rocks beyond the point, you can see yet another small beach, above which are the houses of Westport. If you continue over slippery, seaweed-covered tidal rocks, you will probably get your feet wet. Many varieties of seaweed cover the rocks, mostly red and brown.

As you return you may want to walk along the top of the beach near the cliff, observing the tangled mass of soft chapparel which thrive here. Here is a list of some of the plants:

horsetail fern	lupine
wild mustard	ice plant
chicks and hens	golden poppy
Indian paintbrush	thistle
plantain	blackberry vines
cow parsnip	poison hemlock
coast buckwheat	bracken fern

8

BRUHEL POINT
HEADLANDS AND TIDEPOOLS

This was the territory of the Coast Yuki tribe, which extended along the coast from Rockport to Ten Mile River. It is not known if there was a permanent settlement here. But Mussel Rock, or Lilim as the Coast Yuki called it, was a popular and important seafood gathering place for the Yuki and most of their neighbors. This was aided by the fact that the Coast Yuki maintained friendly relations with most all their neighbors: the Kato and Huchnom to the east, the northern Pomo to the south, and the Sinkyone and Wailaki to the north.

The tribes would come to Lilim to pry mussels, limpets and abalone from the rocks, net surf fish and spear salmon in nearby streams (most small streams on the coast had salmon and steelhead runs before logging and the resulting erosion filled them with slash and silt).

When the white settlers arrived they learned of the sea's bountiful harvest at this place (and others). Mussel Rock has been a popular place ever since then. In the last half of the nineteenth century, there were two towns just south of here, Kibesillah and Newport. Kibesillah, just a mile south, where the Orca Inn is today, prospered until 1885. Sometimes called the parent town of Fort Bragg, Kibesillah met its demise when the lumber mill moved to its present location near the old military post. Unfortunately for Kibesillah, most all of the town moved with the mill, including the post office which had opened just a year earlier. Newport was a smaller town about two miles south of Kibesillah, the shipping port for the lumber town. It also blew away in the dust of the move to Fort Bragg.

The Humboldt Trail from Fort Bragg to Eureka went right along the bluffs at Bruhel Point. At several places along this walk you can see what appears to be the old two-rutted wagon track, especially toward the north end near the point. In one spot the track leads off the edge of the eroded bluff, a victim of the wearing action of the waves.

BRUHEL POINT:

DISTANCE: 1 1/8 mile to 1 3/8 mile round trip.

TERRAIN: Moderately sloping grassy headlands leading to several small coves and extensive rocky tidepool area (at low tide).

BEST TIME: Low tide. Wildflowers best in spring.

WARNINGS: Tidal areas are very exposed to surf. Never turn your back on the ocean. Watch for killer waves. You need a California fishing license to gather mussels or other fish or shellfish. Tidal rocks are very slippery. Wear shoes with good traction and watch your step. Mussel gathering is prohibited during the quarantine season, May 1 to October 31.

DIRECTIONS TO TRAILHEAD: Turn west off Highway 1 to the Vista Point at M. 74.09. This is south of Westport, near a stand of cypress trees. Paved parking.

FURTHER INFO: CalTrans (707) 445-6423.

OTHER SUGGESTION: Just north of Bruhel Point at M. 75.42 is a mile long, narrow dark sand beach at Chadbourne Gulch. The beach is virtually inaccessible at high tide, but is a fine walk at medium to low tide. It is a popular place for surf-fishing and bird watching.

Walk west about 1/8 mile down the grassy headland. Take the left fork near a low windblown cypress. A whole series of points and coves stretch along the coast here. There are a couple to your south, but most of them extend their rocky fingers into the surf to the north of you. If you look north from here to the east side of the highway, you will see round, grassy Kibesillah (Kiba-silla) Hill (650-foot elevation).

If it is not low tide, you can walk along the bluffs heading generally north. But at low tide head out on the tidal shelves here for a look at an incredible variety of intertidal marine life. The trail description will follow the bluffs north, just mentioning the best of the many paths to the tidal flats. From the bluffs west, you are on your own. USE CAUTION.

Just below that windblown cypress on the left path is one easy track to the beach. Directly to the north, a narrow sandy cove extends far inland. There is another path on the north edge of this cove. About 75 feet north, the bluff edge trail rejoins the right fork from the cypress. In another 200 feet an old foundation sits on a point with commanding views north and south.

Just beyond, a deep sub-tidal gulch extends inland about 400 feet. Walk east around this deep channel. Near its northeastern corner is a gravelly clearing strewn with bits of shells, perhaps an old Indian camp. As you walk west, then north to the 1/4-mile point, think of the generations of Native Americans from many tribes who came here every year to camp and gather the sea's bounty.

Another access path leads down to a broad tidal shelf. This one is bisected by a deep submarine channel through which the waves surge, creating a blowhole effect. In another 1/16 mile a very steep path near a windbreak of evergreens leads down to the shore. Avoid this steep trail as there is an easier one just 50 feet beyond.

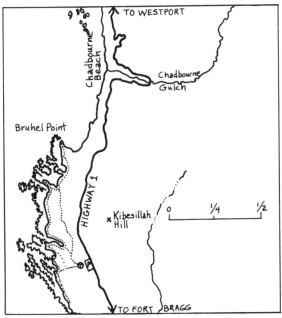

At 1/2 mile you come to a prominent point. Just to its north is a small sandy beach. Directly offshore is a favorite haunt of harbor seals. (Please do not disturb!) A narrow, old road track east of the point is paved with shells. Follow this another 1/16 mile north to the next point and another path to the shore.

More tidal flats lie to the north, but they get progressively harder to reach. From here you can return by the same route to your car or you can angle southeast across the headlands for a more direct route. Or continue north for 1/8 mile to Bruhel Point itself.

Tidal animals commonly seen in the area:

mussel	limpet
barnacle	gooseneck barnacle
purple shore crab	hermit crab
abalone	starfish
sea anemone	spiny sea urchin
turban snail	chiton
giant chiton	Pacific octopus

MacKERRICHER STATE PARK

INCLUDES THE NEXT THREE TRAILS

Just north of Fort Bragg lies a large natural area preserved and set aside for public use within the expanded boundaries of MacKerricher State Park. This stretches from M.69.6 on the north, at Ten Mile River (10 miles from Noyo River), to M.62.7 on the south, less than a half mile from the Fort Bragg city limits. Though this stretch of Highway 1 passes through residential and light industrial areas, an area of 2030 acres lies just to the west, encompassing a variety of habitats: beach, bluff, headland, sand dune, forest and wetland.

The area was originally inhabited by the Coast Yuki and Pomo Indians, who lived a reasonably abundant life from the variety of sea creatures and native plants to be gathered here. It became part of the Mendocino Indian Reservation upon its founding in 1857.

After the reservation was closed in 1867, Duncan MacKerricher settled the land in 1868. He rode to Eureka on the then-new Humboldt Trail to file land claims at the State Land Office in Eureka, paying $1.25 per acre. The MacKerricher family worked the land until 1949, when they gift-deeded it to the State Park system.

In the meantime, in 1916, Union Lumber Co. of Fort Bragg had laid tracks north near the shore all the way to Ten Mile River (and upriver to vast forests of redwoods). The tracks ran where the old logging road runs through MacKerricher Park today (see trail #9). The last train made the run to Ten Mile and back on June 18, 1949. Then the tracks were torn up and replaced by a paved truck road, which was used until the winter of 1982 destroyed about 1/8 mile of road. This allowed the road to be set aside solely for the use of park visitors.

The main entrance to MacKerricher State Park is three miles north of Fort Bragg, at M.64.87 on Highway 1. The trail descriptions start from there. (This is also where you should go if you need information or plan to camp.) There are several other access points to the Park where you can get onto the old logging road, and from there to other trails in the Park. All access is

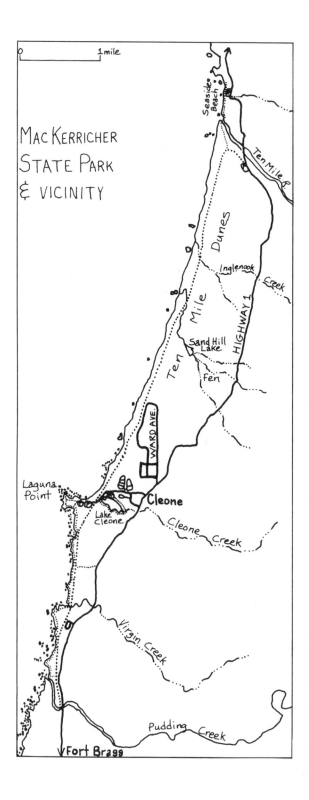

MacKerricher State Park & Vicinity

on the west side of the Highway. They are listed here
in order from north to south:

M.69.65 South end of Ten Mile River bridge.

M.65.20 Ward Avenue.Go west for 1/2 mile to
parking where road makes sharp left.

M.65.06 Mill Creek Drive. Go west for 1/2 mile
into Park.

M.64.87 Main Park entrance.

M.63.70 Virgin Creek trail. Trail leads west from
Highway to join log road.

M.62.70 Old logging road entrance; park near
yellow gate. Now reopened to motorized traffic.

9.

NORTH to TEN MILE RIVER
ALONG THE OLD LOGGING RAILROAD

From the Laguna Point parking lot, walk back to the
gravel road, just west of the underpass. Take the
gravel road to the paved road, then turn left (north).
The elevated road passes above 1500-foot-long
Cleone Beach. At 1/4 mile a side trail on the right
leads to the Lake Cleone parking lot.

Continue north beside low-growing shore pines. At
3/8 mile a horse trail leads east into the wooded
campgrounds of the State Park. At 9/16 mile another
trail leads east into grass-covered dunes. A third trail
leads west to the beach at 3/4 mile. Not far beyond use
caution at a washed-out creek crossing. Yellow and
pink sand verbena, poppies and lupine grow beside
the road.

At 1 1/4 miles a sand dune has formed across the
road, further testament to nature's ability to reclaim
its lands. You may have to walk your bikes around this
obstacle. In another 100 feet you pass the Ward Ave-
nue access point. Up to this point the beach has been
broken by rocky outcrops. But from here north it is
one continuous beach stretching to Ten Mile River.
Wild mustard, reeds and grasses grow beside the
road.

At 1 1/2 miles you reach the section of road which
washed out in the winter of 1982. Cyclists will have to
walk their bikes for a short stretch here, then travel
another short fragment of road to where the road hangs
in ruin at 1 3/4 miles, eaten by the voracious winter

surf after 65 years of use. You must walk your bike through the deep sand of the washout, about 1/10 mile, though it may seem longer. Sand verbena, ice-plant and beach morning glory thrive in the sandy, salty environment.

As you climb back onto the pavement, look north-east into the big forested canyons of Ten Mile River, 4234-foot Cahto Peak visible beyond. Near 2 miles, several log barriers block passage to prevent unwary

---

NORTH to TEN MILE RIVER:

DISTANCE: 5 1/8 miles one way or 10 1/4 miles round trip.

TERRAIN: Paved old logging road, or sandy beach walking.

BEST TIME: Any time.

WARNINGS: Blowing sand can make this miserable in strong winds. Watch for killer waves on beach. Local legend and Indian lore says there is quick-sand on this beach, though I've never found any-thing worthy of the title. Still, the jellified sand might be enough to panic a horse.

DIRECTIONS TO TRAILHEAD: South end: Park at MacKerricher Laguna Point lot, *or* at end of Ward Ave. in Cleone (M.65.20). North end: On Highway 1 (M.69.65) south end of bridge.

FURTHER INFO: Mendocino Area State Parks (707) 937-5804.

OTHER SUGGESTIONS: DUNE WANDERING. The extensive dunes to the east of this route are a great place to wander and discover. Creeks, shell mid-dens, Sand Hill Lake and the Inglenook Fen all lie nestled in this small wilderness.

SEASIDE BEACH lies just north of the mouth of Ten Mile River. When the river is low you can ford it at the mouth and continue north for 1/2 mile on Seaside Beach, or you may access the beach from Highway 1 at M.70.64.

cyclists from plunging off the road's edge. Your road continues north alongside a low area in the extensive dunes on your right. Sand Hill Lake and the Inglenook Fen lie hidden in the dunes to the east. (A fen is a wooded marsh where the soils are composed primarily of decaying vegetative matter. This is the southernmost fen remaining on the Pacific Coast, a prime bird habitat).

At 2 3/8 miles, on the right of your path lie four broad shell middens or mounds. These are the sites of Indian camps, where the coastal tribes cooked and shelled their harvest of shellfish, leaving the large piles of shells to decompose over time. There are many middens scattered in these dunes and elsewhere along the coast. Here they are composed mostly of mussel and limpet shells. A marshy area lies to the east, where the Indians found drinking water.

At 2 1/2 miles you pass an old farm gate on the right. The State Park system has gradually been acquiring old ranch lands which surround the park. The area behind the gate is still private property; please stay out. At 2 3/4 miles you cross a small creek which runs into a small tidal lagoon on your left. Another shell mound lies to the right. Grasses grow on low-lying areas of the mostly bare dunes.

Continuing north, at 3 1/4 miles you pass another farm gate, then cross another small creek with a lagoon. Rushes, willows, lupine, beach sweet pea and Himalaya blackberries grow along the road. The dunes to the right are heavily covered with vegetation. In another 1/8 mile you cross a third small creek.

About 3 5/8 miles the dunes reach their broadest point, extending east for about a mile to a height of 130 feet. They are backed by groves of tall blue gum eucalyptus, the ridges beyond covered with conifer forests. Even though you can see a few houses and ranch buildings at the edge of the dunes, there is truly a wilderness feeling in these dunes. To the north by northwest lie the sparsely settled grasslands of Kibesillah Hill and Bruhel Point. Farther up the coast, on a clear day, you can see the rugged wilderness shoreline of the Sinkyone Wilderness and the Lost Coast stretching to the rounded point of Punta Gorda.

Continue north, with the beach now immediately west of the road. At 4 1/2 miles the road begins a big bend to the right. Tall grass growing on the dunes to the west of the road hides the ocean beyond. At 4 5/8 miles, as the road continues its big bend, is the take-off point for a short walk north to the mouth of Ten Mile River, beyond the rolling grassy dunes.

If you continue on the road, it now heads east, paralleling the river. At 4 7/8 miles you cross the State Park boundary. In another 1/8 mile, a path on the right leads through a stile and climbs the dunes to the north parking area at M.69.65 on Highway 1.

The paved trail continues east under the highway bridge, a favorite nesting place for mud swallows. The road ends in another 1/8 mile, where the construction of a new logging road blocks the old railroad bed. The marshlands along the river and the dense thicket of willows, cypress and vines along the road near the bridge provide another fine bird habitat, a treat for those willing to sit quietly and watch and wait.

If you turn around and head back to the central part of MacKerricher State Park, you will be looking west along Ten Mile River to the sea stacks and sea tunnels at Seaside Beach. As you return through the dunes keep an eye out for birds, other small animals and more Indian shell middens. Think about the time just over 130 years ago when this area (and virtually all the coast) was a wilderness inhabited only by Native Americans and wild animals.

LAGUNA POINT:

DISTANCE: 5/8 mile round trip or 7/8 mile loop.
TERRAIN: Grassy, flat headland leading to rocky point.
BEST TIME: Any time.
WARNINGS: Always watch for rogue waves, especially in winter. Never turn your back on the ocean.
DIRECTIONS TO TRAILHEAD: Enter MacKerricher State Park at M.64.87 on Highway 1 or on Mill Creek Dr. at M.65.06. Go past Lake Cleone (see trail #11) and under the old logging road to the large paved parking lot at the base of the point, facing dark sand Cleone Beach.
FURTHER INFO: Mendocino Area State Parks (707) 937-5804.

10.

LAGUNA POINT
SEALS, WHALES AND SEA LIONS

This short, level walk is very popular for its easy access to the grassy point, tide pools and seal and whale watching. It is a prime habitat for both grassland and shore birds.

The trail leaves from the northwest corner of the parking lot adjacent to Cleone Beach. Walk through the fence and head west over grassy headlands scattered with short, windblown cypress trees. At 1/10 mile is a display about whale watching. About 250 feet beyond you come to another split rail fence. The right fork leads immediately to a small, rocky beach and tide pools. The main trail takes the left fork. Where your trail forks again at 1/5 mile, you again go left. At 3/10 mile, you come to a rough wooden bench designated as "Seal Watching Station."

Directly to your west, at the end of the point, 30 to 40 or more harbor seals lounge on the rocks or play and fish in the surf. They live here year-round. The open water beyond the rocks is prime whale-spotting territory when the gray whales are migrating from December through April. To the right of the point are tide pools where you can see tidal creatures even at a moderately high tide. (Use caution on the slippery rocks.)

You can return directly from here to the parking lot for a 5/8-mile round trip. Or continue the loop around the south end of the point. The trail leads south along the bluff's edge, passing above offshore sea stacks and tide pools, prime shore bird habitat. If you are lucky (or patient) you may see a brown pelican or a blue-footed booby. At 3/8 mile your trail turns southeast with the edge of the bluff. At 1/2 mile you come to another small but protected gravelly beach. From here a side trail heads north to return to the parking lot at 7/8 mile.

You may also continue south along the bluff, in 1/8 mile joining the horse trail which follows the shore south to Pudding Creek near Fort Bragg.

LAKE CLEONE:

DISTANCE: 1 1/3 mile loop.

TERRAIN: Level shoreline of small 15-acre lake, partially forested, partially marshy. Great bird habitat.

BEST TIME: Any time except after heavy rains.

WARNINGS: May be flooded after rains. Be quiet, or you may be the target of a bird watcher's wrath.

DIRECTIONS TO TRAILHEAD: Follow directions in trail #9 but stop at Lake Cleone, just before beach parking area.

FURTHER INFO: Mendocino Area State Parks (707) 937-5804.

OTHER SUGGESTION: You can rent canoes and rowboats at the parking area beside the lake.

11.

LAKE CLEONE
HAVEN FOR TROUT AND BIRDS

Lake Cleone was originally formed as a tidal lagoon of Mill Creek, at a time long ago when the level of the Pacific Ocean was higher than it is now. As the level of the sea receded, the lagoon was flushed by winter storms and eventually became the fresh water, 15-acre lake we see today. Cleone is a Greek word meaning gracious and beautiful. The fine bird habitat around the lake is a permanent home to quail, gulls, hawks, blackbirds and jays. In fall and winter, many migratory fowl stop here: more than 90 species have been identified.

Your trail leads east from the east end of the parking lot. A branch trail soon leads left to Cleone Campground. But take the right fork, continuing along the shore of the lake through willows and alders, with pine forest on your left. As you follow along the north shore two other side trails lead away from the lake, but stay on the shoreline path.

Near the east end of the lake you follow along the edge of a marsh where cattails, sedges and tall grasses provide prime bird habitat. At about 1/2 mile, your trail turns south into the marsh, crossing it by way of several wooden footbridges. Be quiet here, as there are birds all around you, hidden in the tall foliage of the marsh. Only the most quiet will be rewarded with the sounds and perhaps sightings of migratory birds.

After crossing the marsh, the trail turns west and follows the shore of the lake west through a more heavily wooded area. Just short of one mile you cross another small bridge, then continue northwest hugging the shore of the lake. You will soon return to the paved road, where you walk north to return to the parking area.

12.

GLASS BEACH
PUDDING CREEK HEADLANDS
DOWN AT THE OLD DUMP

A paved road heads west from the parking area, beneath an old underpass built of large logs. Wildflowers and berry vines thrive on the 1/4 mile path to the beach. On your left are stacks of Georgia-Pacific lumber waiting to be shipped. (This walk is on G-P land.)

Where the path forks, take either trail. Both lead to coves littered with sparkling bits of glass and pottery worn smooth by tidal action, a mosaic artist's dream come true. For beachcombers this is great territory.

If you want to walk rather than hit the beach, two paths lead north, one winding along the bluff's edge, the other taking a straighter path across lush headlands carpeted with flowers. Both paths lead north for about 1/2 mile before coming to a cliff above the mouth of Pudding Creek. From here, you can return by the trail you came or go east across the logging road, then walk south paralleling the road to your car.

GLASS BEACH
PUDDING CREEK HEADLANDS:

DISTANCE: 1/2 mile round trip with optional 3/4 mile headlands loop.

TERRAIN: Flat headlands leading to convoluted bluffs surrounding old dump site(s).

BEST TIME: Any time you are in town.

WARNINGS: Parts of this beach are particularly exposed to large surf. Use extreme caution when the waves are big. *Never* turn your back on the ocean. Do be aware that this is an old *dump* site. For example, do not let young children put objects in their mouths.

DIRECTIONS TO TRAILHEAD: In Fort Bragg, the northernmost street west of Highway 1 is Elm Street at M.62.0. Go west 2 blocks to parking and start of trail.

FURTHER INFO: Mendocino Coast Chamber of Commerce (707) 964-3153.

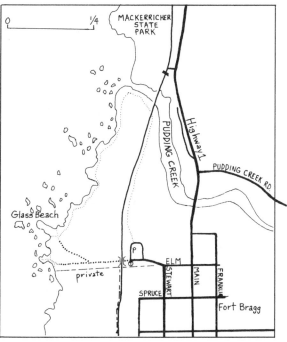

13.

FORT BRAGG HISTORY WALK
AN OUTDOOR TOUR

*In 1855, the United States government established the
Mendocino Indian Reservation, the fourth reservation
in the nation. It extended along the coast from the
Noyo River north to about a mile north of Ten Mile
River and inland to the first ridge, about 25,000 acres
in all. The government attempted to relocate all the
Native Americans from Marin County north to the
Oregon line onto this reservation, though many were
overlooked.*

*In 1857 Lieutenant Horatio G. Gibson was sent to
establish a military outpost for the growing reserva-*

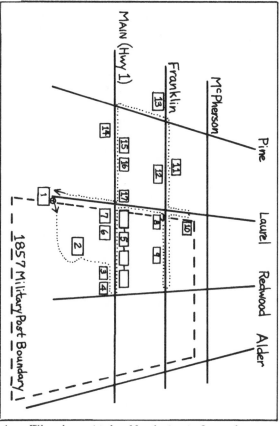

tion. When he arrived at Mendocino in June, there was still no road or trail north to the Noyo River, so Gibson booked passage on a schooner to Noyo. The new outpost was officially begun on June 11, 1857. It was located at the site which is now downtown Fort Bragg. The site was then a beautiful glade, sloping gently west and totally surrounded by dense forest. Lt. Gibson named the post for his West Point classmate and compatriot in the Mexican War, General Braxton Bragg, later a general in the Confederate Army.

The post was abandoned in 1864, as the Native American population was being moved inland to Round Valley, near Covelo, where there is still a reservation today. In 1885 lumbermen established the new town of Fort Bragg at the site of the old fort.

This walking tour guides you through the central area of Fort Bragg, featuring many of its oldest remaining buildings. The tour was developed jointly by the Mendocino County Museum, the Georgia-Pacific corporation and Will Kelsey who are to be thanked for *allowing it to be reprinted here. The original tour has been revised and amended by the author of this book.*

1. RAILROAD DEPOT (est. 1924) is the present home of the California Western Railroad (Skunk). The town's railroad was established in 1885 to serve the Union Lumber Company. By 1904 the rail line provided a link to Alpine, 18 miles east of town, where travelers could transfer to stagecoaches and proceed to Sherwood and the main line Northwestern Pacific Railroad. In 1911, C.W.R.R. connected directly to N.W.P.R.R. at Willits.

You may catch the train here or walk around the railroad yard to view the Skunk (a yellow diesel-powered trolley) and the big steam locomotive. As you walk southeast to the nearby Johnson House, you pass an outdoor display of old logging equipment including the "retired" locomotive "Daisy" (No. 2 on the Caspar Railroad) and two steam donkey engines.

2. JOHNSON HOUSE (est. 1892) was constructed by T. L. Johnson and was later the home of his brother, C. R. Johnson, founder of the Union Lumber Co. In 1912 it became a company guesthouse and was used in this capacity until 1969. This was also the site of the 1857 military post hospital. Johnson House is now a museum run by the city of Fort Bragg. It is open Wednesday through Sunday, 10 to 4. Admission $1, kids under 13 free.

Walk east to Main Street (Highway 1).

3. 319 N. MAIN (est. 1904, now Redwood Empire Title Co.) is the only remaining brick building which survived the 1906 earthquake. Emerging from the side walls are truss rods, installed as reinforcements after the quake.

Walk south to:

4. 303 N. MAIN (est. 1912, now Daly's Department Store) was originally the company store of the Union Lumber Co. A building was constructed here in 1886 and, after surviving the 1906 quake, was replaced by the present structure for $30,000 in 1912.

Cross to the east side of Main and walk north:

5. MAIN STREET (ca. 1890-1950) reflects a blend of commercial architectural styles typical of American towns during the first half of the twentieth century. Historically housing such things as a saloon, general store, restaurant, and shops, this block is also the location of Shafsky's Ben Franklin Store.

Dating from 1892, the Shafsky business is the oldest privately operated mercantile business in town.

Still walking north, across the street is:

6. 353 N. MAIN (est. 1912) has served Fort Bragg as a library since it was built on land donated by the Union Lumber Company.

7. 363 N. MAIN (est. 1912, now the Ten Mile Judicial District Courthouse) was originally constructed as the Fort Bragg Commercial Bank. The building was later taken over by the Bank of Italy, later renamed the Bank of America, which occupied the site until 1960.

Go east on Laurel St. for one block, to the southeast corner:

8. 363 N. FRANKLIN (est. ca. 1890?, now Milvo's and Estates Gallery) was protected from the flames of the 1906 fire by the south-facing brick fire wall. The fire wall was here because the building was a bakery at the time. Only slightly damaged by the tremors, the wall is still visible along the south edge of the building.

Walk south on Franklin to:

9. 335 N. FRANKLIN (est. 1906) was the White House Hotel starting in 1888. It burned down in the fire of 1906 along with virtually every building in a 2-block area. The hotel was quickly rebuilt. Later remodeled into nondescript ugliness, it was restored in 1980.

Walk back north to the corner of Franklin and Laurel. A half block east is:

10. 248 E. LAUREL (est. 1909, now the Footlighters Little Theatre) was originally opened May 9, 1909 as the Sequoia Theatre, Fort Bragg's first conventional movie house. It has been used as a theatre since its construction. Old fashioned melodramas are now performed there every summer.

You are at the eastern edge of the old military post. In the 1890s there was a Chinese neighborhood one block south.

Walk back to Franklin and go north 1/2 block to:

11. OLD FORT BUILDING (est. 1857) was recently relocated from its original location near the southwest corner of the post. Believed to have been the quartermaster's storehouse and fort commissary, this is the last known surviving structure of the Fort Bragg military outpost. It houses a nice little museum. Notice especially the 1863 photographs and painting of

the fort and the 1857 map of the coast, commissioned by the superintendent of Indian Affairs.

Across the street is:

12. 435 N. FRANKLIN (est. ca. 1910?) was constructed as a community hall by electric plant superintendent William Bennett, a local legend. Bennett was a lonely bachelor who created an entire "family" for himself carved from redwood, a wife and five daughters.

There were dances. I remember Mr. Bennett had his dolls . . . and he had them all dressed up. He had a skating rink there and certain nights of the month . . . he would have a dance with all of these wooden dolls (and the whole town). I'm telling you, he was a character.

—from *Mendocino County Remembered: An Oral History*

Walk north to Pine Street. On the northwest corner is:

13. FIRST BAPTIST CHURCH (est. 1912) was constructed for $15,000 and survives as one of the finest examples of California Mission Style architecture in Mendocino County. In 1912 an earlier New England Style church (1890) (not unlike the Presbyterian Church in Mendocino) was moved to the rear of the lot, remodeled, and now remains as the north portion of the present structure. Look for the 1890 church in the central stained glass window of the main floor's south wall.

Walk west to Main, then go south. Across the street is:

14. 435 N. MAIN (est. ca. 1889?) was originally the home of the Fort Bragg Advocate-News, founded in 1889. The newspaper's large rotary press moved several inches during the 1906 quake, but the building was only slightly damaged (though it leans quite severely today).

15. 428 N. MAIN (est. 1908, I.O.O.F./Masonic Hall) was constructed after the earthquake destroyed the large brick building which had previously occupied the site.

16. 418 N. MAIN (est. 1896, now The Restaurant) was one of Fort Bragg's first hospitals. Pelted by bricks during the 1906 temblor when the south wall of the I.O.O.F. Hall collapsed, the building housed the hospital, Dr. Lendrum's office and H.R. Baum's pharmacy.

17. 400 N. MAIN (ca. 1890s, now Fiddles and Cameras). Extensively altered over the years, this building once housed Weller Hall, site of the founding of the Presbyterian (1885) and Baptist (1887) congregations. At the turn of the century, the building housed Shafsky Bros. Workingmen's Cash Store. On Admission Day 1899, an acrobat balanced his way across Main Street on a tightrope stretched between Shafsky's and the livery stable across the street to the west.

This concludes the History Walk. The railroad depot is directly to your west. There are many more historic buildings in Fort Bragg than could be included here. For further historical information, stop in at the library or the Guesthouse Museum across the street.

14.

MENDOCINO COAST BOTANICAL GARDENS
10,000 VARIETIES OF PLANTS

These 17 acres are the coast's premier garden spot. A spectacular mix of exotic and native plants grows here. Over 10,000 varieties of plants thrive in the cool, moist coastal environment of the Gardens.

The main trail to the spectacular ocean bluffs and back is paved, an ideal place for wheelchairs and baby strollers. You can take a quick walk through in about an hour. Better yet, plan to spend the day here with a picnic lunch (or you can eat at the Gardens Cafe near the entrance, March through October). There are many sheltered lawns and meadows where you may spread your blanket and revel in the beauty of the Gardens.

The admission desk is to the right of the Gardens Cafe. (It doubles as a nursery where you may purchase plants.) The paved trail begins here, leading west past many ornamental shrubs and into a beautiful group of cultivated rhododendrons. The grounds are scattered with large Bishop pine, blue gum eucalyptus, tanoak, wax myrtle and redwood. More exotic cultivated trees are present in smaller numbers.

MENDOCINO COAST BOTANICAL GARDENS:

DISTANCE: 2 mile round trip.

TERRAIN: Mostly flat coastal forest and headlands.

BEST TIME: April and May, next best are March and June. Nice any time.

WARNINGS: Please stay off adjacent private property.

DIRECTIONS TO TRAILHEAD: On the west side of Highway 1 at M.59.08 just south of Fort Bragg.

FURTHER INFO: Mendocino Coast Botanical Gardens (707) 964-4352.

FEES:

General	$4.00	
Children	2.00	(Age 12 to 17)
Under 12	free	
Senior	3.00	(Age 60 or over)
Residents	2.00	(Westport to Elk)
AAA members	50¢ discount	
Garden Membership	$10/year individ.	
	$15/year family	

A membership supports the work at the Gardens and entitles you to bring guests at half price.

When the paved path forks, stay on the right fork. Side trails lead to a lily pond and a Mediterranean garden, a heather garden, and Fern Canyon. Signs at the bases of many plants denote common and scientific names of plants to help you identify them.

A little beyond 1/2 mile from the entrance, the path veers left and descends to cross tiny Digger Creek. Native species dominate this part of the garden. Coming up the hill on the other side of the creek, you get a glimpse of the ocean, not 1/4 mile to the west. Notice that the trees do not grow as tall here near the ocean. The farther west you go, the more they are sculpted into irregular shapes by the strong winds which frequently occur here.

The trail passes through a young forest of Bishop

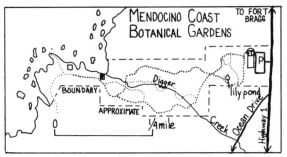

pine, shore pine (actually the same species as the lodgepole pine, the shore pine grows only in the coastal region as a sprawling clump of branches, very different from its high-mountain siblings), Monterey cypress and the scrubbier, indigenous Mendocino cypress.

Just short of 1 mile the trail suddenly opens up onto grassy coastal bluffs scattered with windblown Mendocino cypress. The headlands sparkle with wildflowers most of the year. There is a rest room on your right. Convoluted sea cliffs stretch to the west and north, leading to the suburban sprawl of Fort Bragg. The plume of Georgia Pacific's smokestack billows from behind Todd's Point.

At the end of the pavement, the path forks. You can seek shelter on windy or foggy days in the Cliff House shelter on your right. Or you can walk southwest to a grassy point. An adjacent small rocky hill provides a fine view north and south along the coast. As a third alternative, you can wander south along the headlands on a dirt path. But this path soon turns away from the coast and leads onto private property.

Your return trail follows the route on which you came for the first 1/4 mile, going right at the first paved fork to return by the loop trail. A bit farther, the Canyon Rim trail branches off to the left, a more primitive dirt alternate paralleling the main trail.

Continuing on the paved path, take the left paved fork, descending into another section of Fern Canyon. (The right fork leads to a service area.) Walk down to and across the creek, rapidly leading back into the giant cultivated rhododendrons. As you meet the path you came out on, stay on the right. Your trail immediately veers right onto the last leg of the loop.

Ahead you may stop at the lily pond on your left. There is a small bench from which you can enjoy the water lilies. If you are quiet, the frogs may perform for you. The pond contains imported bullfrogs with a deep basso croak, easily distinguished from the higher pitched, screen-door-squeak croak of the local frogs. If you are lucky, one or more of the frogs may be perching atop a lily pad.

About 150 feet beyond the pond a gravel detour leads left through a grassy clearing east of the pond. (People with wheelchairs or strollers may stay on the paved path.) The paths meet ahead at the drought-resistant Mediterranean Garden. In another 200 feet you come to the exit.

JACKSON STATE FOREST

Jackson State Forest was established in 1947 when the State purchased most of the land of the Caspar Lumber Company. This 50,200 acre forest stretches from Fort Bragg to Mendocino and inland for up to 18 miles. This extensive tract of land is used for timber harvesting and forestry studies. It is also open to public recreational use.

A network of dirt logging roads crisscrosses the State Forest. Many older roads are closed to vehicle traffic and suitable for hiking, riding or mountain biking. Numerous primitive campsites lie in the north and east portions.

This book includes five trails in Jackson State Forest: #15 — North Fork of the South Fork Noyo River, #16 — Chamberlain Creek Waterfall and #17-2, part 2 of the Mendocino Hiking and Equestrian Trail, which follow directly. The two other trails appear later in the book since they are in the south part of JSF: #24 — Part 3 of the Mendocino Hiking and Equestrian Trail and #25 — Forest History Trail at the Mendocino Woodlands.

Contact the State Forest headquarters for more information and the location of other places you may hike.

15

NORTH FORK of SOUTH FORK NOYO RIVER

SECLUDED REDWOOD CANYON

This hike, and the dirt road leading to it, follows the main line of the Caspar Railroad to Camp One, then follows a spur line into and up the canyon of the North Fork of the South Fork of Noyo River. This lumber railway originated in the early 1870s in Caspar, originally ran on wooden "rails" (due to a shortage of steel caused by the Civil War) and was pulled by horse and oxen. In 1875 the Caspar Railroad brought the first steam locomotive to the coast.

The Railroad gradually extended its line north and east over the years, seeking new forests to cut. All the activity was south of the Noyo River until a new tunnel was dug in 1903. This 1000-foot tunnel ran from Bunker Gulch on upper Hare Creek into the South Fork of the Noyo drainage. The tunnel ran beneath Highway 20 near your turnoff.

Camp One, where the egg-collecting station is now, was the biggest and longest lasting camp in the woods for the Caspar Lumber Company. Located at Camp One was a small town; bunkhouses for single men, bungalows for families, a store, a cookhouse, an ice plant, a school, an engine house and switching yard for the cluster of engines used in the woods. It was occupied until the railroad was abandoned in 1945.

Along Road 360 leading north were other more temporary logging camps (now mostly car camps) where smaller woods operations were centered. They were numbered in the order in which they were established. By 1915 Caspar Railroad reached Camp 8, just before the trailhead. Over the next nine years the line built and logged its way up the canyon where the trail is today. When the area was logged out in the late 1920s, the rails were removed and laid elsewhere. Wood was cheap at the time, however, and crossties and trestles were mostly left to rot in the woods, where you will see them on this hike.

Parking at the right fork's shady dead end, walk 75 feet back to the junction, and take the steep road now

NORTH FORK of SOUTH FORK NOYO RIVER:

DISTANCE: 4 miles round trip.

TERRAIN: The bottom of a steep, wooded stream canyon to near the headwaters.

ELEVATION GAIN/LOSS: 900 feet+/900 feet−

BEST TIME: Late spring and all summer.

WARNINGS: Prime habitat for poison oak. Use extreme caution when driving back roads to trailhead. Narrow and winding road doubles as the Mendocino Hiking and Equestrian trail (see #17-2). May be impassable in rainy season. Avoid in deer-hunting season, August to September; watch and listen for gunfire.

DIRECTIONS TO TRAILHEAD: Turn east off Highway 1 onto Highway 20 at M.59.8, just south of Fort Bragg. Go 5.9 miles to Road 390 on left, leading downhill by some redwoods. In .3 mile, take the right fork. About a mile from the highway, you pass a remnant of an old railroad trestle. You then pass several spur roads on the left. Stay on main road. Just 3 miles from the highway you come to the Noyo Egg Collecting Station (where spawning salmon and steelhead are stripped of their eggs for hatcheries). Just past the hatchery at 3.2 miles you come to a big intersection. Take Road 360 heading east. Stay on this road past a junction at 4.4 miles where it turns into Road 361 (Road 360 makes a sharp left). Road 361 continues past several campgrounds until it forks at 7 miles. You may take the right fork and park here or continue up a steep hill on the rough left fork for .2 mile to road's end. The author recommends the former choice and the trail description starts there. (It is hoped that the State Forest will block off the last portion to car traffic).

FURTHER INFO: Jackson State Forest (707) 964-5674.

on your right. The roadbed narrows in the next 3/16 mile, ending near a small footbridge across a tiny side stream. Cross the bridge, passing a rustic sign mark-

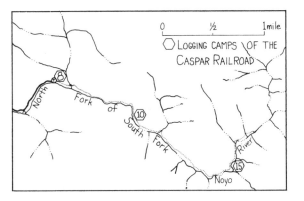

Logging Camps of the Caspar Railroad

ing the trail. The trail switchbacks twice to climb above the steep cutbank of the creek. As the trail proceeds along mostly level ground, notice that the environment on your left is much drier than the streamside environment.

At about 5/16 mile you enter redwood forest. Douglas iris, redwood sorrel, western windflower and slink pod grow in abundance along the trail. At 3/8 mile you come to a fork. You may take either path as they rejoin not far ahead, having descended steeply to the creek.

At 7/16 mile you are again near the old logging trestle which you will follow for most of the hike. Notice that it is not made of fancy cut lumber, but of rough cut poles which were probably the first trees cut here, then quickly slapped into place. At 1/2 mile you are right alongside the trestle. Ferns, huckleberry bushes and poison oak grow out of its rotting wood. Old rusted spikes are exposed. A few of the cross ties are still in place.

About 5/8 mile the trail passes along a steep cutbank. The forest here consists almost entirely of bay laurel which grew in place of the redwoods which were cut. You will soon re-enter deep redwood forest. Crossing a small bridge, the old trestle is still on your right.

A little more than 3/4 mile beyond the trailhead grow healthy young redwoods upwards of 3 feet in diameter. You cross several more roughhewn redwood bridges. Near 13/16 mile the trestle (across the creek) widens into a broad platform that may have been a landing for the old logging operations. Large trees which must be only about 60 to 70 years old grow through the platform.

Your trail then climbs by about 40 roughly-built wooden steps to an open grassy clearing at 7/8 mile. You quickly switchback to the right and drop back down to the bottom of the canyon. At 1 mile, you are walking on top of the old railroad bed. As you jog left where the trestle again crosses the creek, a bright patch of columbine blooms in spring and early summer. Notice that the streamside environment becomes drier from here to the end of the trail.

For the next 1/4 mile the trail mostly stays atop the old railroad bed. In this stretch many of the original cross ties are still in place. Grass, wild rose, berries and poison oak grow at trailside. You cross a small bridge over a tributary, then again follow the track bed. Near 1 5/16 miles two old apple trees grow above the creek on your right, the site of an old homestead.

At 1 3/8 miles the trail veers left as the trestle shoots diagonally across the canyon. The next section of trail has suffered some erosion. First you come to a washout; go downhill towards the creek to get around the gully before you. Then, after climbing a steep short hill, you are at the top of a large slide. Watch your step! It is a steep drop on the right. Just beyond in a small drainage grow scouring rush, wood fern, sword fern and wild strawberries. The trail continues to climb to high above the creek in tanoak forest.

About 1 11/16 miles, you descend to within sound of the creek, then to an old road. The environment here is cool and lush with healthy redwoods. At 1 3/4 miles you climb more steps, then follow the lay of the land into a shady northeast slope.

Just short of 2 miles from the trailhead, the trail drops by 10 steep steps to trail's end alongside the stream. A log there provides a place to rest and have a snack to ready you for the hike back.

At one time this trail continued upstream to meet a different logging road to the east. It was closed off several years ago when the headwaters above the current trail's end were logged. The State Forest plans to reopen the trail eventually to join the road system near Three Chop Ridge, not far from the waterfall (see next trail report).

CHAMBERLAIN CREEK WATERFALL:

DISTANCE: 1/4 mile to 1/2 mile round trip.

TERRAIN: Short steep walk into creek canyon with virgin redwoods.

ELEVATION GAIN/LOSS: 85 feet+/85 feet−

BEST TIME: Late winter or spring, when waterfall is in full glory (after a big rainstorm is best); a pretty spot at any time.

WARNINGS: The trail is quite steep but mercifully short. This trail can be slippery, especially when wet but even when dry.

DIRECTIONS TO TRAILHEAD: From Highway 1 south of Fort Bragg, turn east onto Highway 20 at M.59.8. Go east to M.17.4. Just past the Chamberlain Creek bridge, turn left onto Road 200. You come to a big intersection at 1.2 miles, where Road 200 goes left. Climb gradually on Road 200, then more steeply to 4.7 miles from Highway 20. There the road widens with parking for 4 cars on the left shoulder. A wooden railing leads downhill.

FURTHER INFO: Jackson State Forest (707) 964-5674.

OTHER SUGGESTION: At M.17.3 on Highway 20, just west of the Chamberlain Creek bridge, turn left and park by the steam donkey engine visible just north of the Highway. The CHAMBERLAIN CREEK DEMONSTRATION FOREST trail leaves from there. It consists of a short loop below the parking area or a longer loop uphill from your car. The interpretive brochure generally must be picked up at the State Forest Office in Fort Bragg, at the corner of Main and Spruce Streets.

16.

CHAMBERLAIN CREEK
WATERFALL WALK

For the author, this virgin grove will always be known as the Glenn Watters Memorial Grove. This was a special place for Glenn, who would go out there in

*most any weather in his Birkenstocks. It was Glenn
who first told the author what a fine place it is.*

A wooden railing and 30 steps lead downhill from the
parking area. You continue descending steeply
(watch your step), then turn right into cool, young
growth forest. At 1/16 mile, you drop by two switchbacks into a moist environment where rhododendrons, redwood sorrel and sword ferns thrive. After
one more switchback near a big rock, you descend
into virgin redwood forest near the creek.

Follow the trail beneath two large fallen redwood
logs and the waterfall is suddenly before you. At the
base of the 50-plus-foot falls grow five-finger and
other ferns. Also growing in this moist pocket are
trilliums, false solomon's seal, and fragrant vanilla
leaf (3 large wedge-shaped leaflets).

The virgin redwoods extend west into a side canyon. You may cross the creek on a large fallen log, or
you may ford the creek near the base of the falls if
the water is not too high. In 200 feet you come to a
fire ring and picnic spot. From there a small path
leads west up the side canyon, though you must
scramble over and under fallen logs. The path continues beyond 1/8 mile but becomes very rough at
that point.

Take your time climbing up the steep hill back to
your car.

MENDOCINO HIKING & EQUESTRIAN TRAIL
PART ONE: SHERWOOD ROAD

Just beyond the junction a sign warns: "Road not maintained during winter months." Heed the warning; as late as April or May large mud holes may lurk around the first bend. These recur intermittently along the first 1/2 mile. Then the road starts to climb, gaining 550 feet in the next mile. There are good views to the east and south.

A spur road branches to the left, the first of many. You should be careful along this entire route not to mistake these spurs for the main ridge route. Notice that spurs are *generally* rougher and *often* lead downhill, while the main route generally does not change suddenly.

At 3/4 mile the road becomes very steep and rough. You soon encounter more deep mud holes (or their dried up remains). At 1 2/10 miles, after another steep climb, you gain the top of the ridge. You can see the drainages of Pudding Creek (foreground) and Ten Mile River to the north. Another very steep climb brings you to a level top at the 1 1/2 mile point. Just beyond, a clearcut on your left allows you to look west for a bird's eye view of town and the surrounding coast.

The road goes downhill past some large redwood stumps for the next 1/4 mile, then climbs again to the 2-mile point at M.6.5. One very steep and muddy uphill section can be circumvented by taking a duff covered old road track on the left, which quickly returns to the main route. The road levels briefly, again followed by a downhill stretch marked by a steep and rutted sharp right turn, wrapping around a large redwood.

Adjacent to the redwood is a large stump with a flat mossy top. This is a pleasant place to rest, especially on a warm day. Unfortunately this spot (and much of Sherwood Road) is strewn with cans, bottles, broken glass, toilet paper and other signs of uncaring humans. It seems that *some* people cannot tolerate being surrounded by nature without cluttering it with

MENDOCINO HIKING & EQUESTRIAN TRAIL
Part One:

DISTANCE: 26 miles one way. (From Company Ranch Road, Sherwood Road junction to eastern trailhead, near Sherwood Indian Rancheria). Part of 44 mile Mendocino Hiking and Equestrian Trail.

TERRAIN: Old dirt stagecoach road up and down along rambling ridges. Area has been severely logged.

ELEVATION GAIN/LOSS: 3780 feet+/1320 feet− (to Willits another 900 feet−).

BEST TIME: Late spring to late fall.

WARNINGS: May be impassable in rainy season. Open to motor vehicles, although not heavily traveled. Still you should watch and listen for motor traffic. Surrounded by and passing over private timber lands. Do not trespass. No water available except at Coon Camp and near Sherwood Peak. Watch and listen for hunters and "recreational shooters." Deer season begins the second weekend in August and runs to end of September.

DIRECTIONS TO TRAILHEAD WEST END: Turn east off of Highway 1 at Oak Street (M.61.3), near the center of Fort Bragg. Exactly one mile east, at Fort Bragg city limit, Oak becomes Sherwood Road. The mileage markers count from here. Go 4.5 miles more to unmarked intersection of Sherwood Road and Company Ranch Road. *Park off road.* (Though you can drive farther, road quickly becomes steep and rough beyond this point.)

DIRECTIONS TO TRAILHEAD EAST END: Turn west from Highway 101 at north end of Willits onto Sherwood Road. Go 8 miles to Octagon House. Parking is a problem at the eastern trailhead.

FURTHER INFO: Mendocino County Road Department (707) 964-2596. For map, see page 18.

ENVIRONMENTAL CAMPS: Coon Camp is located at M.11.00. Wanhalla Camp is at M.27.50.

signs of their presence. This pathological compulsion to litter cuts across all segments of human culture (even some hikers, God forbid!). Don't you be one of the bad guys! Even better, do your part by picking up some of the litter to carry out with you. In this way you can thank Mother Nature for enriching your day.

Dropping to the most level portion of the route so far, you pass M.7.07 (2 1/2 miles from the trailhead) and stay on the level beyond M.7.25. Here you have views both north and south through the forest. Then you descend slightly to a large clearcut with an expansive view to the north and northeast (the tall mountain is Cahto Peak). From here you can also see two large logged areas, the left one a "selective cut", the one to the right a clearcut. The next 1/4 mile of trail is open and sunny with spots near the road for picnics and sun bathing. Please do not trespass onto the adjacent timber lands. Along the road grow Douglas iris, redwood sorrel, wild strawberries, sword ferns and an occasional calypso orchid.

At 3 3/4 miles from your starting point (near M.8.25), after a short climb, the road bends left around another clearcut. This stretch is mostly level with short drops and climbs to 5 1/4 miles.

Then you begin another descent, dropping for the next 1/2 mile. In spring 1986, this section of road (and intermittently from here east) was blocked with fallen trees from winter storms. One could always find a way around these barricades, but bikers would often have to walk or lift their bikes around or over the logs.

At 5 3/4 miles your route climbs again gradually for the next 3/4 mile. Then, near M.11.00, the road descends slightly around a large logging scar on the right. Just beyond a saddle near the 7 1/2-mile point, there is a clump of redwoods by the road on your right. This is Coon Camp, a tiny camp provided by Georgia-Pacific as an overnight stop or picnic spot. The rules are: one night stay only, no fires, hikers and equestrians only, use the outhouse. There is a covered spring box just east of camp; the water is brackish but potable. Please keep horses away from the spring.

After Coon Camp, the trail climbs for the next 1 3/4 miles. There is a seasonal stream just 1/4 mile beyond the camp with very cold and fresh water; it is better than the spring at camp, if it is still flowing. Two other seasonal streams also flow from the mountain on the left. At M.14.00, about 9 1/2 miles from the trail-

your climb levels, then descends slightly. The peak to your left rises to 1550 feet above sea level.

Most of the next stretch of Sherwood Road is level. Do not mistake the many side roads along this stretch for your trail. Most of them are blocked by a gate or a pile of dirt. The trail continues along the ridge.

At M. 18.25 you pass the last county road marker. The county road continues, wandering back and forth from the north side of the ridge to the south side and back again. It is mostly well shaded by the forest on this stretch. Tanoak and ceanothus are prevalent.

Approximately 23 miles from Fort Bragg, you arrive at Wanhalla Camp on the south side of the road. The camp is in an open area overlooking the canyons of the Noyo River and the wooded ridges to the south. It is provided courtesy of Louisiana Pacific Corporation, which owns the surrounding lands. You are permitted to have a fire here, as long as you build it in the fire box provided. Carry out your trash please. A 1250 gallon water tank provides drinking water (if it has been filled recently). Be sure to keep the tap turned off.

As you leave Wanhalla Camp, Sherwood Road climbs generally upward toward Sherwood Peak across L-P lands designated as a tree farm. This continues for 4 1/2 miles to the L-P boundary about 28 miles from Fort Bragg. Just beyond the boundary is the site and remains of an old lumber mill, one of many in these hills which were abandoned in the 1950s as lumber production was centralized.

Just over one mile from the mill, you come to a clear fresh water stream which bubbles from the mountainside just above the road. You can fill your canteen year round here with the sweet spring water. You have less than 3 miles to go.

In less than a mile you come to a level area on land owned by the Barnum Timber Company. They use it as a hunting camp, but you are not allowed to camp here nor to trespass on the Barnum land. You are just below the 2650 feet summit of Sherwood Peak. The views from the road in this area are spectacular, as Sherwood is the highest peak near the coast between Cahto Peak near Branscomb (4234 feet) and Cold Springs Peak near Philo (2736 feet). To the south lie many heavily timbered ridges lining up to the horizon. To the west are more ridges, extending to the glistening Pacific on a clear day.

From the level area near the peak, the road drops first gradually, then more steeply by sharp curves. Watch for motor traffic again as you are approaching the populated Sherwood Valley near Willits. Just about a mile from the summit the road levels, then comes to Octagon House, the official end of the trail. If you watch carefully for traffic you may continue the eight miles into Willits, mostly downhill. It is even better if you have arranged to be picked up at the eastern trailhead.

17-2.

MENDOCINO HIKING & EQUESTRIAN TRAIL
PART TWO: HIGHWAY 20 TO SHERWOOD ROAD

After crossing Highway 20 at M.8.08, the trail turns west and parallels the highway briefly, then turns right and heads downhill on a logging road. At 3/10

MENDOCINO HIKING & EQUESTRIAN TRAIL
Part Two:

DISTANCE: 7 7/10 miles one way.

TERRAIN: From ridge to river canyon to ridge to canyon, then climbing to a third ridge, traversing many habitats. This is the most arduous section of the Mendocino Hiking & Equestrian Trail.

ELEVATION GAIN/LOSS: 1505 feet+/1825 feet−

BEST TIME: Late spring to late fall.

WARNINGS: Bridge across Noyo River at Company Ranch is removed in winter. Trail is sometimes closed by logging operations; inquire at State Forest Office. North portions of trail cross private land by permissive use agreements. Stay on trail. Portions of trail are open to motorized traffic. Watch and listen for gunfire, especially deer season: August and September. Watch for poison oak.

DIRECTIONS TO TRAILHEAD SOUTH END: Turn east off Highway 1 at M.59.8 (just south of Fort Bragg) onto Highway 20. Go east to M.8.08. There a logging road goes downhill on the left.

DIRECTIONS TO TRAILHEAD NORTH END: Turn east off Highway 1 at Oak Street (M.61.3), near the center of Fort Bragg. Go 5.5 miles east to unmarked intersection; Sherwood Road continues ahead, Company Ranch Road (on the right) is the trail.

FURTHER INFO: Jackson State Forest (707) 964-5674.

mile, a trail sign points right. You leave the logging road here for the old wagon road to Camp One. This wooded path descends north for 7/8 mile, coming to flat ground near the Noyo Egg Collecting Station. Here salmon and steelhead are stripped of their eggs in order to restock other streams with these endangered species. Nearby are several campsites in the area called Camp One. (It was the first logging camp on the railroad line of the Caspar Lumber Company).

From here the trail follows Road 360 north alongside the North Fork of the South Fork of the Noyo River. Watch carefully for motorized traffic for the next 2 1/2 miles as you will be walking or riding *on the road.* You pass two pleasant campsites along this stretch: Wagon Camp and Tin Can Camp.

At 2 miles from Highway 20, after a short but steep hill, the stream crosses to the right side of the road. Just beyond, you (and Road 360) take a sharp left and head up Brandon Gulch. (Road 361 is on the right, leading to the North Fork of the South Fork trail.) After the turn, you should be heading northwest.

You come to another junction at 2 4/5 miles from Highway 20. Go left here on Road 362, climbing 800 feet in 8/10 mile to Riley Ridge, where you meet Road 1000. Just across from the junction the Hiking and Equestrian Trail descends west by northwest, leading to the Noyo River in 2 more miles, a 1000-foot descent.

This section of trail crosses the property of Georgia-Pacific Company; stay on the trail and do not trespass. You pass through an old homestead site, with an apple orchard on your right, then continue descending along Sointula Creek.

At the bottom of the hill you intersect with a logging road. Turn right here, following the road for 150 feet across a bridge over the North Fork of the Noyo River. (The bridge is seasonal — generally May to September.) Then cross the tracks of the California Western Railroad (Skunk) and bear right briefly to Company Ranch Road, named for the old ranch here, once owned by the Union Lumber Company (G-P's predecessor).

Take the Company Ranch Road uphill for 1 1/2 more miles, climbing 510 feet. Again you should watch for motorized traffic. At 7 7/10 miles from Highway 20, you will top the ridge and come to the junction with Sherwood Road and the northernmost segment of the Mendocino Hiking and Equestrian Trail, which heads east from here. (Fort Bragg is just 5 1/2 miles to the west on Sherwood Road.)

For Part 3 of the Hiking and Equestrian Trail, see Jackson State Forest South, near Mendocino (#24.)

JUGHANDLE ECOLOGICAL STAIRCASE:

DISTANCE: 5 1/2 miles roundtrip.

TERRAIN: Through creek canyon, then climbing gently over ancient marine terraces which demonstrate geology and flora variations of the region, through tall forest on ancient dunes, then leading to stunted pygmy forest on flat ground.

ELEVATION GAIN/LOSS: 280 feet+/280 feet−

BEST TIME: Spring to fall.

WARNINGS: May be impassable after heavy rains.

DIRECTIONS TO TRAILHEAD: Turn west off Highway 1 just south of Jughandle Creek bridge at M.56.10.

FURTHER INFO: Mendocino Area State Parks (707) 937-5804. Ranger-led hikes on Saturdays in summer.

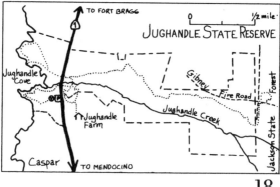

18.

JUGHANDLE ECOLOGICAL STAIRCASE

SHOWPLACE OF COASTAL EVOLUTION

Jughandle Creek was set aside as a state park in 1978. It had long been recognized as a prime example of the ecological history of the Mendocino Coast, not to mention one of the best preserved showplaces of coastal landscape evolution anywhere in the Northern Hemis-

phere. Its importance became recognized primarily through the pioneering work of botanist Hans Jenny, who identified the uplifted marine terraces which occur near the creek along with the resulting varied botanical habitats.

The ecological staircase consists of five wave-cut terraces, each about 100 feet higher and 100,000 years older than the next. The youngest terrace, at the start of the hike, emerged from the sea about 100,000 years ago. The oldest terrace is more than 500,000 years old. Each terrace was raised above the younger one as a result of the tremendous tectonic forces which have built the coast ranges, as the Pacific (offshore) continental plate collides with the North American (onshore) plate.

Though it is difficult to imagine such powerful forces as you hike the coast's forests and grasslands, to the trained eye the evidence of this tectonic uplifting can be seen at many places up and down the Mendocino Coast. This hike up Jughandle Creek passes through some of the clearest examples of the progressively uplifted marine terraces, helping us all to better understand and recognize these powerful forces which shaped, and are continuing to shape, the western edge of our continent.

You may purchase the interpretive brochure for this hike for 50 cents at a vending machine at the trailhead. The brochure is highly recommended, although this is a wonderful hike even if you do not follow the brochure.

The trail heads west from the parking lot onto the grassy coastal prairie, where more than a dozen species of wildflowers bloom from April through June. The trail loops clockwise around the headlands for 1/2 mile. At the terrace edge you look over the cliff to offshore sea stacks, then north into bowl-shaped Jughandle Cove and its broad sandy beach.

You then head east following the bluff's edge above the cove, passing a steep trail down to the beach. (No dogs beyond this point: prime wildlife habitat). Continue east through mixed conifer forest, then under the highway bridge. About 100 feet beyond the bridge, take the left fork, making a steep descent to the creek, about 3/4 mile from the trailhead. The creek is tidal to just above this point. You may see it flowing uphill if the tide is rising. (Down by the creek,

a wonderful little side trail leads upstream. Known as the Doree Diamond trail, this spur leads through a beautiful swamp on a narrow boardwalk for 300 feet before continuing on drier ground into tall Sitka spruce forest.)

You cross the creek on a sturdy new bridge. An arrow on the far side points out the trail north, away from the creek. Before climbing back up to the first terrace, you come to a stand of red alder. The blood-red sap of this tree was used as a dye by many Native American tribes. In the shade of the alder a sign warns of poison oak, though it was not prevalent here in 1986. If you back too far from the sign you will encounter the sharp pain of stinging nettles. Notice these plants and avoid them on this and other trails.

The trail climbs the hill back toward the highway, passing poison oak, then sticky monkeyflower, beach morning glory and Scotch broom. At the top of the hill, a trail forks left, leading to the headlands north of Jughandle Creek (see #18A.)

The main trail turns right and east through mixed pine forest and grasslands. This is a good area for spotting deer.

About one mile from the trailhead you walk through a small tunnel of brush, climbing gradually. A big blackberry patch is on your left. The trail steepens as you climb from the first to the second terrace. Here grand firs begin to mix with the pines. At 1 1/8 miles you pass through the clearing of an old homestead before entering a tall forest of Sitka spruce, grand fir, western hemlock and Bishop pine. Lichens, redwood sorrel and sword ferns cover the forest floor.

At 1 1/4 miles the forest floor becomes dominated by a carpet of false lily of the valley, lush green plants with heart-shaped leaves and tiny white flowers. As you climb gradually up to the second terrace, other plants begin to appear on the forest floor: first bear grass and salal, then wax myrtle mix with the false lily of the valley. Then Labrador tea (with pungent white flowers) appears. Soon red huckleberries grow on your right, quickly followed by red alders, evergreen huckleberries, pink rhododendrons and tanoak.

Near 1 3/8 miles you begin to see Oregon grape (holly-like leaves, yellow flowers in May). As you enter a drier habitat, manzanita and wild rose occur.

An old fence line runs north and south, perpendicular to the trail (#13). You are leaving the old homestead and entering what was once timber company land. The area ahead was logged in 1961. As you walk on, notice how well a natural area can recover from logging in 25 years.

Just 30 feet beyond the fence the trail forks. Take the right fork, continuing through the young growth forest, dominated by Bishop pine and young hemlocks. Near 1 1/2 miles you come to a partial clearing, created when the logged area was burned over to clear slash (logging debris). There is a rest bench here. Notice how the hardwood species and grass intruded on the forest after the fire. Eventually the conifers will grow to dominate the intruders.

Notice the orange-brown soils of the next section of trail. This hardpan soil is one of the first steps in the creation of the pygmy forest environment. Eventually the hardpan will become so thick that most plant roots will not be able to penetrate it.

Continuing east you soon cross under a power line. This was the right of way of the old Caspar Railroad, which ran from the mill at the mouth of Caspar Creek and up Jughandle Creek from here in the early 1870s. Due to a shortage of iron caused by the Civil War, the first "rails" were made of wood. The timber laden cars were first pulled by oxen until it was realized that animal power could not do the job. In 1875 the coast's first steam locomotive was brought in pieces by schooner from San Francisco, reassembled and immediately put into service on the wooden rails. The engine, dubbed "Jumbo", raced along at a top speed of 10 miles per hour, a great improvement over the oxen. About 1880, after Caspar Lumber Company bought more timber land to the north, a huge wooden trestle was built to span the deep chasm of Jughandle Creek. The trestle, located where the power line crosses today, was 1000 feet long and 146 feet high. At that time it was the world's largest wooden railroad bridge. It carried many huge loads of timber before folding like an accordian in the 1906 earthquake.

At 1 3/4 miles from the trailhead, you find redwoods growing on a rise to the left of the trail. The rise is an ancient sand dune, created 200,000 years ago by waves and wind at the base of what is now the third terrace. The sandy, well-drained soil of the dune creates an excellent growing environment, where the redwoods and Douglas fir grow tall and healthy (especially in contrast to the hardpan of the pygmy!). You can see the sand underlying the forest duff near where the trail turns left and climbs onto the dune.

A different group of shade loving plants grow on the forest floor here: sword fern, trillium, the tiny pink starflower, clusters of red clintonia blossoms (replaced by dark blue berries [inedible] in summer) and an occasional calypso orchid. For the next 1/4 mile you climb gradually onto the third terrace through the tall forest. Many more clintonia line the trail. Mature Bishop pines join the redwoods and firs.

The trail now follows the ridge of the dune through beautiful forest on the rolling terrain around you. Rhododendrons line the trail. This is also good country for wild mushrooms, many of which are poisonous and should not be touched.

At 2 1/4 miles you come to a stand of big western hemlocks (#20), which love moisture and thrive on less well-drained soils. Deer ferns grow on the forest floor here. They look somewhat like sword ferns, but their leaflet edges are smooth. You continue along the crest of the ancient dune, a steep drop into Jughandle Creek canyon on your right.

Near 2 1/2 miles you are climbing uphill, entering the transition zone between the well-drained dune soils and pygmy forest. You may notice that the conifers are neither as tall here nor as vigorously growing. Less demanding hardwood species like tanoak and wax myrtle are competing with the conifers for the available light, soil and moisture. The hardwoods do better in hardpan soil than do most conifers.

About 200 feet beyond #22, your trail turns sharply left and leaves the forest for transitional pygmy, a drastic change in the landscape. The trail here is a bit confusing: go north on a broad fire road. You cross another more-traveled road which runs east-west (a dirt extension of Gibney Lane).

Within 100 feet the trail leaves the fire road, veering right into the heart of the pygmy forest. Typical of pygmy soils, this area does not drain well; there may be standing reddish brown water after rain, highly acidic (from the soil) and known as pygmy tea. A Bolander pine grows on your left. The Bolander is a variation of the species Pinus contorta, which grows as lodgepole pine (straight and tall to 80 feet) up to 11,000 feet in the Sierra Nevada, and as shore pine (dense and scrubby) near the coast north to Alaska. The Bolander variation occurs only on pygmy soils and seldom grows much taller than this 16-foot-tall example.

Two other species limited almost entirely to pygmy soils also occur here. A Mendocino cypress grows on the right of the trail opposite the Bolander. Fort Bragg manzanita is low growing with small shiny leaves, not easily confused with its bigger cousin, hairy manzanita, which also occurs in the pygmy forest.

Though the preponderance of plants here grow to only about 8 feet, with a smaller number of trees growing to 20 feet, there are a few larger Bishop pine and Mendocino cypress up to 50 feet. The roots of these trees have broken through the pygmy hardpan to reach underlying pockets of nutrients.

At 2 3/4 miles you are approaching the end of the trail. At #31 you see stressed Bishop pines, struggling to survive in the pygmy soils. The pines here are infested with dwarf mistletoe (not related to the Christmas-time parasite), a family of parasites which saps the vigor of live conifers. Trees are generally stressed or damaged before being infested with this parasite. But the dwarf mistletoe often is the last straw which kills off the tree.

In just 100 feet you come to #32, the last item in the interpretive brochure. The drainage ditch before you shows the layers of soil underlying this pygmy bog: thin humus, thick leached podsol, reddish brown and iron-rich hardpan, then beach sand and gravel underlaid with graywacke sandstone bedrock. Imagine trying to grow your vegetable or rose garden in such soils. That is what many coastal residents have to do.

From #32, turn right, following the ditch downhill for about 150 feet to the Gibney fire road. There you continue west another 250 feet, then turn left on the north-south fire road back to the big forest and the main trail going west above the creek canyon. It is about 2 miles to your car.

18A.

JUGHANDLE ALTERNATE TRAILS:

THE PINE BEACH/MITCHELL POINT TRAIL heads west through Monterey and Bishop pines onto grassy headlands, leading to a tiny beach and

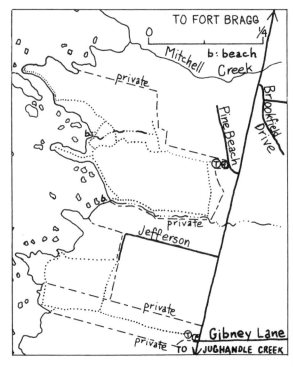

JUGHANDLE ALTERNATE TRAILS:

DISTANCE: 1/2 mile to 1 1/4 miles round trip each.

TERRAIN: Coastal grasslands leading to bluffs and small pocket beaches.

BEST TIME: Spring for wildflowers, but any time is nice.

WARNINGS: Do not trespass on adjacent private property.

DIRECTIONS TO TRAILHEAD: All on west side of Highway 1 at the following mileposts:

Pine Beach/Mitchell Point trail: M.57.6

Bromley beach trail: M.57.3

North headlands trail: M.56.75

South headlands trail: M.56.10

FURTHER INFO: Mendocino Area State Parks (707) 937-5804.

OTHER SUGGESTIONS: THE BEACH TRAIL branches off main trail north of parking area, leading down to the beach of Jughandle Cove.

CASPAR HEADLANDS STATE RESERVE lies just south of Caspar Creek. You must first obtain a permit from the State Park headquarters to use this coastal access. They will give you a map indicating the precise location of access trails through private property to the bluffs and adjacent tide pool areas.

Mitchell Point beyond, a prime whale watching spot. Flowering plants include cotoneaster, beach strawberry, iris, poppies and lupine. (3/4 to 1 1/4 mile, round trip)

THE BROMLEY BEACH TRAIL heads west over open headlands to ocean bluffs with offshore sea stacks. A small beach lies just to the north. (1/2 to 3/4 mile round trip)

THE NORTH HEADLANDS TRAIL goes west from the Highway (or you may get onto it from the Ecological Staircase trail) through pines onto open headlands just north of Jughandle Cove. (3/4 mile loop)

THE SOUTH HEADLANDS TRAIL is the first part of the Ecological Staircase trail, but it is a fine short walk by itself. (1/2 mile loop)

RUSSIAN GULCH STATE PARK

INCLUDES THE NEXT THREE TRAILS

Russian Gulch State Park was established in 1932. Just two miles north of the town of Mendocino, the 1245 acre park includes varied habitats: coastal headlands and pine forests, a verdant stream canyon and wooded ridges.

Local Indian lore told of seeing trappers with large ships landing at this cove in the late eighteenth century. They fit the description of the Russian fur traders, thus the name Russian Gulch.

A fine network of trails winds through the park, three of which are described in the following pages. Several other trails are mentioned in the text.

19.

WATERFALL LOOP

LUSH CANYON TO A WATERFALL

Here you can bicycle, wheelchair or walk through a lush riparian canyon unhindered by motorized traffic. The 2 1/2-mile-long (5 miles round trip) paved bike path is one of the most beautiful in California, allowing an intimate visit with a small coastal stream and its verdant habitat. To go on to the waterfall, one must continue on foot. Nevertheless the trail remains gentle, affording a nonstrenuous 6 1/2 mile outing. Add an extra mile to continue over the ridge beyond the waterfall, for a somewhat more arduous but still pleasant hike.

The trail starts just east of the campground, where the main park road is blocked to motorized traffic. The

WATERFALL LOOP:

DISTANCE: 6 1/2 miles round trip or 7 1/2 miles semi-loop. (Wheelchairs and bikes can only do the first 2 1/2 miles, 5 miles round trip.)

TERRAIN: Gentle creek canyon, heavily forested, leading to 36-foot waterfall.

ELEVATION GAIN/LOSS: To falls: 220 feet+/220 feet−. Full loop: 500 feet+/500 feet−. Bike path only: 90 feet+/90 feet−.

BEST TIME: Late winter or spring, but any time is nice.

WARNINGS: Watch for poison oak.

DIRECTIONS TO TRAILHEAD: Turn west off Highway 1 at M.52.95, then left to park entrance. After kiosk go left again under Highway and into canyon. Parking: 0.9 mile from kiosk.

FURTHER INFO: Mendocino Area State Parks (707) 937-5804 or at the kiosk.

OTHER SUGGESTIONS: THE NORTH TRAIL climbs the north side of the canyon from campsite #24, coming back to the main trail near the picnic area at the east end of the bicycle trail. (2.5 miles each way)

THE NORTH BOUNDARY TRAIL leaves from the park headquarters and climbs high above the canyon to follow the park boundary for about 3 miles before coming out on Road 409 at M.3.35.

THE SOUTH TRAIL heads south from the Group Camp, climbing to the south canyon rim, then descending to the east end of the park road near campsite #30, a distance of 3/4 mile.

paved trail winds alongside the stream in the bottom of this lush canyon. The canyon is heavily forested, though it was once much more so before the early loggers took the virgin trees. Now the conifers (redwoods, grand fir, western hemlock and Douglas fir) dominate the sides of the canyon, while deciduous

93

water-loving trees (alders, willows, big leaf maple, tanoak) dominate the canyon bottom. Lichens and ferns abound here as do other forbes (water-loving plants) like ferns, nettles, berries and wildflowers.

The first mile is nearly flat. Then in the second mile you climb slightly as the creek picks up speed. The trees get larger as you proceed up the canyon. At 2 1/2 miles the paved path finally loops to its end. Beneath the redwoods sit three picnic tables where you may rest. Cyclists will want to lock their bikes here to continue up the canyon. Wheelchairs might get a bit farther but the terrain quickly gets rougher and steeper.

Just 75 feet beyond the picnic area, the North trail leaves the canyon heading west by northwest, a good alternate return route for those on foot. Continue another 75 feet to the start of the waterfall loop. Take the left fork, noticing that Russian Gulch Creek also forks here. Wild rose and trillium begin to appear near the junction. In 1/8 mile the trail climbs by steps as the canyon becomes steeper. Near a wooden bridge just beyond grows a clump of columbine.

A little farther, as a second wooden footbridge crosses a tiny tributary, rhododendrons appear beneath the dense forest. You climb a series of stone steps.

Approximately 3/4 mile from the trail fork, you come over a rise and the falls are before you. Dropping over a flat shelf of hard franciscan rock, the falls tumble 36 feet, sending clouds of spray into the air. Notice how many plants grow in the mist at the base of the falls. The sun seldom penetrates the deep forest here to light the waterfall. Photographers do best with fast film, though early afternoon may bring a few patches of sunlight to the falls. If the day is hot, you might want to venture into the spray at the base of the falls.

You can return by the same trail for the shortest, easiest hike. Or you can continue the loop up over the ridge south of the falls. You should at least climb the trail switchbacking to the top of the falls for a look at the stream above the falls. Bear grass, huckleberry and rhododendron form a garden through which the placid stream wanders before plunging over the brink. At the top of the falls, the trail is carved out of the bedrock in a series of stone steps.

For the next 1/8 mile the trail parallels the placid stream. The sound of the falls roars behind you. As the trail switchbacks up and away from the creek, a small footpath drops back to streamside amidst a gentle garden (nice blanket picnic spots). Climbing onward, you do not see the falls again, except for a glimpse at the westernmost switchback, about 1/4 mile after leaving the falls. Rhododendrons now begin to dominate the forest understory, mixed with low, holly-leafed Oregon grape and tanoak trees.

At 3/8 mile beyond the falls you top the ridge. The trail stays atop this wooded ridge for another 5/8 mile. Your high ground trail traverses the headwaters of several feeder drainages of Russian Gulch Creek. The wetter habitat here brings more dense underbrush. Just about a mile beyond the falls, the trail drops abruptly through brushy forests into the deep canyon on the south. This is the fork of the creek which you left at the start of the falls loop. The roar of the creek below grows louder as you drop the 1/4 mile to streamside and the return trail.

Go northwest here, returning to the loop junction in 3/8 mile. Total loop is about 2 1/2 miles, although the sign claims 3 miles. That makes 7 1/2 miles total from the trailhead. Return down the canyon to your car.

```
┌─────────────────────────────────────────────┐
│              BLOWHOLE WALK:                   │
├─────────────────────────────────────────────┤
│                                               │
│  DISTANCE:  1/5 mile round trip to blowhole   │
│    or 5/8 mile semi-loop.                     │
│  TERRAIN: Gradually sloping grassy head-      │
│    lands with giant blowhole, wave tunnels    │
│    and natural bridges.                       │
│  BEST TIME: Spring for wildflowers. High      │
│    tide for best blowhole action.             │
│  WARNINGS:  Stay out of the blowhole —        │
│    dangerous! Stay back from the very edge    │
│    of the cliff.                              │
│  DIRECTIONS TO TRAILHEAD: Turn west off       │
│    Highway 1 at M.53.00, 2 miles north of     │
│    Mendocino. Turn left again to State Park   │
│    entrance kiosk, then go .1 mile. Turn      │
│    right and go .25 mile to parking and       │
│    trailhead.                                 │
│  FURTHER INFO: Mendocino Area State           │
│    Parks (707) 937-5804.                      │
│                                               │
└─────────────────────────────────────────────┘
```

20.

BLOWHOLE WALK
TUNNEL RIDDLED HEADLANDS

It is just 1/10 mile to the venerable old blowhole of Russian Gulch, but the entire point is riddled with wave tunnels and natural bridges. From your car, walk 1/10 mile west to the fence around the blowhole. A blowhole is a collapsed wave tunnel, worn by strong tidal action over millenia to a point where tidal pressure causes the water to surge into, and sometimes to gush out of, the abyss. While this blowhole is too large to erupt like a geyser, watching the power of the wave action here is still impressive. This giant is over 100 feet in diameter, 400 feet in circumference and about 80 feet deep. The inlet is at the southwest corner. If the surf and tide are high, go to the sea cliff directly south of the blowhole and marvel at the raging waves which surge into the blowhole tunnel.

Walk farther west from here onto the narrow point. Looking back toward the blowhole, you can see that the ocean has nearly worn another tunnel into the blowhole from the west. Across the small cove to the south is a sturdy natural bridge. Yet another wave tunnel undercuts the point beneath your feet. Land's end is a bit farther, about 1/6 mile from your car. More wave tunnels and natural bridges are visible to your north, northeast and east. On the grassy headlands around you Douglas iris bloom starting in February, soon joined by sea thrift, beach strawberries, ice plant, yarrow, poppies and a profusion of other wildflowers.

Retrace your steps to the foot of the point, then turn south. You can walk out to the head of the southern point if you like. From here, return by walking along the south edge of this headland. Great views of Russian Gulch to the east and Mendocino headlands to the south can be seen. It is a short walk uphill to the parking lot. A pleasant picnic area is 1/8 mile east.

21.

SOUTH HEADLANDS LOOP
FOLLOWING THE CROOKED SHORE

The trail climbs a hill to get above the canyon, then follows the canyon rim leading west. Soon you come to the junction with South trail (which goes east above the canyon) amidst grand firs and lush vegetation. Walk south to a eucalyptus grove beside the Highway. Take the right fork which leads under the bridge. Soon the trail forks again. Your return trail is on the left. Take the right fork, leading through Bishop pine forest growing right to the cliff edge. Douglas iris grows tangled with poison oak and berries on the forest floor. At 3/8 mile from the trailhead, you come to a small wooded point with commanding views of Russian Gulch. In another 1/8 mile, after a brief uphill stretch, you can turn left to return to the trailhead (3/4 mile total) or turn right for a longer loop.

If you go right, it is 1/8 mile along the cliff edge to a paved cul de sac, an old stretch of Highway 1. If you follow the paved road for 400 feet, you come to another headlands trail on the west, this one leading to an open grassy headland, very different than the wooded headland to the north. This full double loop is about 1 3/8 miles.

DISTANCE: 3/4 mile semi-loop or 1 3/8 mile double loop.

TERRAIN: Lush wooded headlands with commanding view of Russian Gulch, then grassy headlands with views to south.

BEST TIME: Anytime.

WARNINGS: Stay back from the cliff edge.

DIRECTIONS TO TRAILHEAD: Follow directions in #20 but go straight at junction after kiosk for .2 mile. Turn right and park at the Group Camp. Trailhead on south side of road.

NOTE: No fee parking is available along old Highway 1. Turn west off Highway 1 at M.52.00. Go .4 mile.

FURTHER INFO: Mendocino Area State Parks (707) 937-5804.

From the paved road take the first trail south of the cul de sac. Walk generally west through grass and low brush with scattered Monterey pines. After 1/10 mile you are beyond the trees on a flat grassy headland. Another 1/10 mile brings you to the tip of the point. From here you can look north to the entrance of Russian Gulch. The Gulch itself hides behind the wooded point from which you just walked.

From here the loop goes south, for about 100 feet paralleling exposed tidal rocks. At the south edge of the point, Mendocino headland stretches out before you. The westernmost point is Goat Rock. The north edge of the village of Mendocino is visible, but nearly all the "old" town lies hidden on the south (sunny) side of the point. From here follow the south headland back to the paved road, about 1/4 mile.

The return hike to the group camp is about 1/2 mile.

TOWN OF MENDOCINO

Mendocino was once known as "The Jewel of the North Coast." Though its sawmill has been gone for fifty years, the town survives today as a haven for artists and a popular tourist destination.

Mendocino was founded in 1852 when a shipload of San Franciscans came north to find the immense redwood forests on the coast. They established the first successful sawmill on the Mendocino Coast, shipping the redwood lumber south to supply California's gold rush. The first mill was located at the tip of the point, near the blowhole. (A tidal-powered mill had been started earlier that year at Albion, but was destroyed by killer waves in the winter of 1853.) In 1854 a larger mill was built for Mendocino, located 1/2 mile upriver from Big River Beach. It operated nearly continuously until it was shut down in the 1930s.

The town was originally known as Big River or Meiggsville, but the first post office opened in 1858 with the name Mendocino. Many woodsmen and other settlers came to Mendocino from New England, helping to establish the town's distinctive New England style. By 1877, the township of Mendocino had the highest population (3100) and property valuation in Mendocino County, $1.5 million, one quarter of the county's total valuation.

After the sawmill closed, the town teetered on the brink of oblivion for a few years. Its biggest fame during that time came from being the location for the filming of two Oscar-winning movies, Johnny Belinda *starring Jane Wyman (1948) and* East of Eden *starring James Dean (1955). The mansion used in* East of Eden *burned in 1956. In 1959, the Mendocino Art Center was established on that site, giving new life to the town as an artists' community.*

Today Mendocino and its magnificent coast are renowned far and wide. Crowds of visitors strain the systems of the old town, especially during summer months and on weekends. When Mendocino is crowded, parking and traffic become a problem. Since it only takes about ten minutes to walk across town, it is best to plan on walking after you find a precious parking spot. (What the town really needs is a giant underground parking garage and a ban on cars along Main Street.)

Water and public toilets are also scarce in Mendocino. The town has always had a water shortage (hence the many water towers). When the crowds descend in summer the problem becomes acute. Notice the two public rest rooms on the map; there are no other public rest rooms.

Mendocino has an active cultural life for its small size. Many shops (including two bookstores) and art galleries provide shopping and browsing opportunities. Plays and musical events occur year-round.

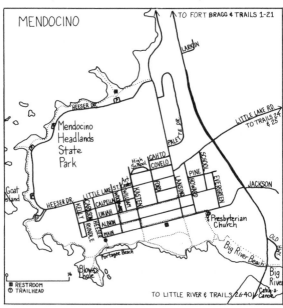

22.

MENDOCINO HISTORY WALK
JEWEL OF THE NORTH COAST

Today Mendocino thrives as a busy artistic and recreational community. As you walk its streets, think back to the booming lumber town which created most of what you now see.

Reflecting the times in which it grew, the town of Mendocino had a two-tiered social structure. The elite owned the mill, banks and mercantile stores. They were well aware of their superior wealth and education and did not socialize with the working men. The loggers and mill workers worked long hours six days a week, then played hard when they brought their pay

MENDOCINO HISTORY WALK:

DISTANCE: 3/4 mile loop.

TERRAIN: Mostly level on paved streets.

BEST TIME: Any time, although town is crowded in July and August, and on most weekends.

WARNINGS: None.

DIRECTIONS TO TRAILHEAD: There are three streets which enter the town of Mendocino from Highway 1:

Lansing Street at M.51.50

Little Lake Street at M.50.85

Jackson Street (which leads to Main Street) at M.50.55

The History Tour starts at the Presbyterian Church on the east end of Main Street.

FURTHER INFO: Kelley House Museum, 45007 Albion Street, (707) 937-5791.

to town. At the peak of the lumber boom there were nineteen saloons in town. The east part of town was known as Fury Town because of the mood on Saturday night.

By 1865 Mendocino's population had reached 700. The 1880 census counted 3100 people in Big River Township (which included the coast from Caspar to Albion). Today the population is about the same as in 1880.

1. MENDOCINO PRESBYTERIAN CHURCH (est. 1868) is the oldest continuously-used Protestant Church in California. Built of locally-milled redwood, the building faces south because the original coast road passed between the Church and Mendocino Bay. Also on the south side of the Church is the EIDSATH HOUSE (est. 1909), now home to the Mendocino Study Club, a privately-run library. It may have the best view of any library in the U.S.A.

Across Main Street, slightly to the east is:

2. THE McCORNACK HOUSE (est. 1882, now the Mendocino Village Inn) — Also known as the Doctor's House, this two story white house was built by

Dr. William McCornack and later served as a residence for three other doctors. The original exterior ornamentation was recently restored.

The next house to the west is:

3. LANSING HOUSE (est. 1854?, now private) was built by Captain David Lansing, one of the town's first settlers. A sea captain and superintendent of shipping operations at the Mendocino Saw Mill, Capt. Lansing imported redwood lumber from San Francisco to build the house because early lumber from the local mill was rather roughly milled. Lansing installed the state's first railroad line in 1853 to facilitate ship loading on the point. It was 180 feet long at the start, soon expanded into a maze of tracks on the point.

Walk west on Main Street, passing Howard and Lansing Streets and the old Ex-Lax Building on the corner (now the Melting Pot), the next building is:

4. KELLEY HOUSE (est. 1861, now a museum, open Friday through Monday, 1-4 p.m.) was built by William H. Kelley, who ran the company store after arriving in 1852. The Kelley family acquired much land over the years. They preserved the original character of this two block area until the 1970's. Then it was bought by Mendocino Historical Research, Inc. The large lot includes the house, lawn and gardens, the water tower and the duck pond.

Walk west to the duck pond — directly behind, one street back is:

5. MacCALLUM HOUSE (est. 1882) was built as the residence for Alexander MacCallum, a junior partner of William Kelley, when he married Kelley's daughter Daisy. An 1882 article in the *Mendocino Beacon* marveled at the house's modern amenities: "Hot and cold water can be had in three different places, and there is a bathroom with sprinklers overhead for family use."

On the other side of Main Street, 100 feet west is:

6. FORD HOUSE (est. 1855, now a State Park building, public restrooms to the east) was always known as the Company House, because the Mill superintendent lived there. The west section was built first. The original kitchen and dining room were underground (for reasons unknown). The first boy born in Mendocino was born to the Ford's in this house. There being no school in those years, the first grammar school classes were also held here.

Walk west on Main Street for 200 feet to:

7. MENDOCINO HOTEL (est. 1878) was one of eight hotels along Main. The back part of the building is even older, having been moved to the back of the lot when the new addition was built in 1878. The Bever brothers operated it as the Central House for 25 years. It later became the Mendocino Hotel. It had a pool table, tavern and cheap rooms until 1975.

Continuing west along Main Street, at the end of the block is:

8. JARVIS-NICHOLS BUILDING (est. 1874, now several businesses) was built by (or for) Lauriston Morgan, whose father died trying to establish a shipping point at Needle Rock near Bear Harbor (see trail #3) in 1868. Morgan established a "new and elegantly fitted up store" at this location in 1874, according to a local newspaper report. In 1870 the fire which destroyed this and 25 buildings to the west of here started at this location. After the fire, the center of town moved eastward. By 1879 this building became the Jarvis-Nichols store, which served the community for 39 years. As late as 1960 it was still a store, owned by Chet Bishop. It was seen in the movie *Johnny Belinda*. Around the corner is the Gallery Bookshop which was started in the market's old store room in 1962.

Across Kasten Street is:

9. BANK OF AMERICA (est. 1908) was originally the Bank of Commerce. It was restored in 1985. Before the 1870 fire, this was the location of the Chung Kow Wash House. Clothes were hung out over Kasten Street to dry.

Walk north one short block to Albion Street. Go left, then 300 feet. On your right is:

10. JOSS HOUSE (KWAN TI TEMPLE) (est. 1882) One

of the few old Chinese temples left in California, this tiny shrine was a focal point for the coast's Chinese community. The first Chinese are said to have come to the area when their gold rush-bound junk, way off course, was shipwrecked near Caspar. By the 1880's, 250 Chinese lived in Mendocino, about 600 total on the Coast.

Walk west to the next cross street (Woodward). After you turn right, on your left is:

11. CROWN HALL (est. 1901) was built as a social hall for the Portuguese community. It is now used for community events of all kinds.

Walk east on Ukiah Street for 350 feet to:

12. LISBON HOUSE (a.k.a. PAOLI HOTEL, est. 1881, now various shops) served the community for years with lodging, a hard liquor bar (for men only) and a ladies' parlor where soft drinks were served. It was refurbished in 1984.

13. ODD FELLOWS HALL (est. 1878, now Gallery Fair) was built for $2000. It has been beautifully restored.

In the next block on the right, next to the windmill is:

14. KASTEN-HEESER HOUSE (est. 1852, now part of the Mendocino Hotel) was the first house built of sawn lumber in Mendocino. Modified from its original salt box style, over its first century it was home to several prominent pioneers: William Kasten, William Kelley, William and August Heeser.

Across the street and east slightly is:

15. THE BEACON BUILDING (est. 1870?, still the *Beacon* headquarters and various shops) was the site of the second bank north of San Francisco, established 1870. In 1877 William Heeser started the *Mendocino Beacon*, a weekly paper which covered the entire coast.

Continue east on Ukiah Street to:

16. BAPTIST CHURCH (est. 1894, now Corners of the Mouth Natural Foods) William Kelley built it for his wife Eliza, who wanted a church of her own faith. It was only used until 1914, but has been lovingly maintained, like the other Kelley properties.

Continue east to the corner of Lansing Street. On the left is:

17. MASONIC TEMPLE (begun 1866, completed 1872) This is Mendocino's most famous building. It was built by Erik Albertson as fast as Lodge finances

would permit. He carved the top statue of Father Time and the Virgin out of one chunk of redwood.

This concludes the Hip Pocket History tour. If you would like to learn more about Mendocino's history and landmarks, go to the Kelley House Museum one block south. They conduct guided history walking tours every Saturday at 11 a.m. (weather permitting). Also available at the Kelley House is a booklet with a more extensive walking tour, *A Tour of Mendocino*. It covers 30 buildings, including the large old houses along Little Lake Street.

23.

MENDOCINO HEADLANDS STATE PARK
BLUFFS, BEACHES & HISTORY

This walk is a quick getaway from the crowds on busy days in the town of Mendocino. Or in the off-season, especially on weekdays, you may have the entire head-lands to yourself. The headlands are a wild garden of escaped domestic plants: hedge rose, calla lilies, cab-

MENDOCINO HEADLANDS STATE PARK:

DISTANCE: 1 3/4 miles round trip.

TERRAIN: Mostly level, grassy headlands bordered by steep cliffs with paths to two pleasant beaches.

BEST TIME: Spring for flowers, but any time is good.

WARNINGS: Stay back from the edge of dangerously steep cliffs; every year people are hurt and/or trapped because they venture too close to the edge or do not heed the tides. Don't let it be *you!* Don't let rising tides trap you at the base of impassable cliffs. Watch for poison oak in the tangle of vegetation on the bluffs.

DIRECTIONS TO TRAILHEAD: See directions for Trail #22, Mendocino History Walk. Go to the very west end of Main Street, where there is more parking available. The trail description starts from there, at the corner of Main and Heeser Street. Other trails access the same headlands at Main and Kasten and at Main and Lansing Streets.

FURTHER INFO: Mendocino Area State Parks (707) 937-5804.

OTHER SUGGESTIONS: MENDOCINO HEADLANDS WEST AND NORTH: From the Main and Heeser Streets trailhead, you may also go west to explore the headlands on the ocean side of Mendocino. Go right at the first trail junction. The blowhole, surrounded by a low fence, is on the point south of the trail. You may continue west, then north, paralleling Heeser Drive on a footpath near the bluff's edge. In just over one mile you come to the north rest rooms, the park boundary not far beyond. A small path there leads down to a tiny beach. Return as you came. Or you may head east to Lansing Street where a right turn brings you back to town in 3/8 mile. Another option is to ride bicycles along Heeser Drive, following the same headlands.

bage family plants, creeping myrtle, mint, cotoneaster, Scotch broom and nasturtiums.

Like the town, the bluffs and bay are full of history. The Pomo Indians had a village here, which they *called Booldam (big river). California's first railway was built on the point in 1853. This was one of the first doghole ports, where ships were loaded with freshly cut redwood lumber using an apron chute located near the blowhole on the point. This was a dangerous task even without the often treacherous sea conditions. One story tells of a lumber schooner being sucked into a 700-foot wave tunnel in high seas, never to be seen again. (The crew jumped to safety.)*

Another story claims that the blowhole on the point was connected by an underwater passageway to a deep pool about 2 miles up Big River. This submerged tunnel was said to be the source of mysterious moaning sounds heard for years by people crossing the prairie between Little River and Mendocino. After many seasons of floating timber down Big River to the mill, the deep hole upriver became filled with debris and the moaning stopped.

The first large and continuously producing sawmill on the coast was at Mendocino. It operated for 86 years to make Mendocino the coast's leading community. It provided a large share of the redwood which built and rebuilt San Francisco.

If you are hungry and want to eat before your walk, tasty, handmade Mexican food is available at Lu's Bay Kitchen, just 300 feet east of your starting point on Main Street. Or you may work up an appetite on your walk and end up at Cafe Beaujolais, one block north of the Presbyterian Church, for a delicious breakfast or lunch.

From the corner of Main and Heeser Streets, a trail heads south through the fence. In just 100 feet, the trail forks. The right fork leads to a blowhole on the point and connects with the Headlands West and North trail (see OTHER SUGGESTION). The trail in this report takes the left fork, quickly coming to benches near the bluff's edge and a stairway to little Portagee Beach.

The trail turns left and heads east along the bluff. You follow the route of an old logging railway. What may have been the first rail line in California was built on this point in 1853. Teams of oxen pulled the cut lumber to the point for loading onto ships. In places you can see the old crossties on the path.

At 1/6 mile, wooden steps lead through a small gully, coming to a side path on the far side (leads north to Main and Kasten Streets). As you continue east the trail forks. You can choose the right fork, which wanders close to the bluff's edge or the more direct left path along the hedge roses, both heading generally east toward Big River Beach. On the right path you come to a small point at 1/4 mile. Two old Bishop pine snags stand on the bluff's edge. Your trail then takes a sharp left. You pass through a small dip at 3/8 mile, then come to another junction. (The left path leads uphill to the corner of Main and Lansing Streets.)

Take the right fork to the beach, continuing east through old Bishop pines. At 1/2 mile the trail starts to descend toward the beach. On your right grow Indian paintbrush, sticky monkeyflower, beach morning glory, poison hemlock and poison oak.

You descend more steeply, coming to the beach at 5/8 mile. The fine light sand of Big River Beach extends east for about 1/4 mile. On the left grow sand verbena and bush lupine. A marshy area lies at the base of the cliff. Though State Park property ends at the highway bridge, the beach continues east along the north side of the river.

Return to the headlands by the same path, then take whichever path you choose into town.

24.

MENDOCINO HIKING & EQUESTRIAN TRAIL

PART THREE: LITTLE LAKE ROAD TO HIGHWAY 20

The signed trailhead lies next to a redwood on the north side of the road. The well-beaten, mostly level path leads north through mixed forest of Bishop pines and firs. You pass several side trails, but stay on the obvious main trail. Hairy manzanita, rhododendrons, Labrador tea, evergreen huckleberries and young western hemlocks line the trail.

At 1/4 mile you swing right (east) and meet a forest road, which your trail follows for the next section. (Watch for motorized traffic.) Soon a small, brown trail sign confirms that you are on the right trail. Your trail swings left there, then soon turns right again, meeting a bigger road (Road 770) just

MENDOCINO HIKING & EQUESTRIAN TRAIL
Part Three:

DISTANCE: 10 miles one way.

TERRAIN: Through tall forest, then pygmy, drop-ping to headwaters of Russian Gulch before climb-ing along ridges with fine views.

ELEVATION GAIN/LOSS: 1320 feet+/990 feet− (net gain 330 feet).

BEST TIME: Spring to fall (except deer hunting season August through September).

WARNINGS: Watch and listen for motorized traf-fic. Occasionally closed due to logging; inquire at Jackson State Forest before taking trail. Watch and listen for gunfire.

DIRECTIONS TO TRAILHEAD: South end at Men-docino, turn east off Highway 1 at M.50.85 onto Little Lake Road. Trail starts at M.2.78. Or, from the north end, from Highway 1 at M.59.8 go east on Highway 20 to M.8.08. For the north portion of the Hiking and Equestrian Trail, see #17.

FURTHER INFO: Jackson State Forest (707) 964-5674. For map, see page 18.

ENVIRONMENTAL CAMP: Berry Camp is located 8.7 miles from the south end of the trail. This is an old camp where settlers from all over the coun-ty came to pick and can berries in the summer. (Camp closed through summer 1987.)

short of 1/2 mile. Little Lake Road is about 200 feet south of this junction.

You turn left here and quickly drop into a canyon, then climb steeply up the other side. At 3/4 mile the road levels. Here you enter transitional pygmy forest (dwarf trees mixed with a few taller conifers) where you find Fort Bragg manzanita, Mendocino cypress and Bolander pines. In the next 1/2 mile there are 3 spur roads on your left; stay on the main road (inter-sections marked with brown trail signs).

Just beyond 1 1/4 miles you come to a bigger intersection. Continue on Road 770, heading north-east through the pygmy forest.

At 2 miles from your trailhead, the trail leaves the

road on which you have been traveling and takes the left spur, plunging steeply into the canyon of Russian Gulch. (Cyclists may have to walk this heavily rutted stretch of road.) The habitat becomes more moist as you come to the sound of running water; more hemlocks, rhododendrons and thimbleberries line the road. You quickly come to a crossing of the headwaters of Russian Gulch Creek at 2 1/8 miles. You might want to rest here and look down the gulch at tall, mixed redwood forest.

Beyond the creek the road climbs quickly to a "T" intersection with another unmarked road (Road 760). As of June 1986, equestrians have to detour to the right here because the bridge to the left is unsafe for horses. This detour soon comes to Little Lake Road where riders continue to Road 409 and turn left to rejoin the main trail. Hikers and cyclists should take the left turn, quickly coming to the ravaged log and dirt bridge where caution should be taken in crossing.

Continue northwest on the mostly level road, passing a big mudhole at 2 1/2 miles. Just beyond, the trail turns right and heads uphill through dense young-growth forest. (At this point you are about 1/2 mile upstream from the Russian Gulch waterfall.) Your trail continues climbing eastward for the next 1/2 mile, up a steep hill to meet Road 409 on the ridge at 3 1/16 miles from your trailhead. (For a shorter loop of 5 3/4 miles, cyclists can turn right here, proceed to Little Lake Road and return 2 1/2 more miles to the trailhead.)

The trail continues on the north side of Road 409, bending around a big log, which keeps four-wheeled vehicles off the trail. You head generally northeast through tall mixed forest of redwood, firs and Bishop pine. Your route quickly turns east as you meet the old ridge road. Follow that to 3 1/4 miles where a sign at the junction indicates that you take the left fork. Between you and the sign grow deer ferns; note the smooth edge of the fern's leaflets, unlike the serrated edges of the otherwise similar sword ferns seen nearby.

Continue northeast on the ridge, descending slightly. At 3 1/2 miles, head-high bracken ferns grow along the trail. The trail forks just beyond. The trail marker indicates the left fork. You descend to a big landing where pampas grass and 20-foot-high ceanothus grow. Your trail continues east, then drops

down to another landing. Not far up a short hill you come to Little Lake Road, the old pioneer route you follow north. The trail sign calls it Little Lake-Sherwood Trail, 4.7 miles to Berry Camp. The Mendocino Woodlands Road junction is just 50 feet northeast.

From the 4-mile point (watch for motor traffic from here on) you climb moderately through tall forest. At 4 1/4 miles you can look west into the heavily wooded Caspar Creek drainage, the ocean beyond. Mile 4 1/2 finds you climbing steeply, ascending the next 1/2 mile to near the top of 1240-foot-high Great Caspar. Also known as Observatory Hill, this high point was used as a lookout to coordinate logging operations in the gulches below, also to watch for wildfires.

From mile 5, your road stays on the ridge, Big River drainage on your right and Caspar Creek on the left as you head generally north. The road climbs, then drops, then climbs again, repeating this pattern for the next 4 miles along the ridge. Side roads lead off to the left and right, but stay on Road 408.

At 8 3/8 miles you come to a junction with Road 500. The trail continues east on 408, but go right for 3/4 mile to Berry Camp if you plan to camp. (Berry Camp will be closed through summer 1987.)

Just beyond M.11.00, Road 408 veers right, but your trail takes the left fork, dropping down to the crossing with Highway 20 at 10 miles from the trialhead. Use extreme caution crossing the busy highway. The trail continues with Part Two of the Mendocino Hiking and Equestrian Trail (see trail #17-2).

DISTANCE: 4 miles semi-loop.

TERRAIN: Up a creek canyon through redwood forest to a peak, then down through logged areas.

ELEVATION GAIN/LOSS: 900 feet+/900 feet−

BEST TIME: Spring for wildflowers, but anytime is good.

WARNINGS: As of publication time you must sign a liability waiver as you enter the Mendocino Woodlands. (Deep pocket insurance problems have forced this non-profit camp organization to do this.) Poison oak and stinging nettle occur along the trail. Though the trail is well graded, it is a steep climb to the top; don't overdo it.

DIRECTIONS TO TRAILHEAD: Turn east off Highway 1 at M.50.85 onto Little Lake Road. Go 5.65 miles to where Little Lake becomes a dirt road. Turn right on unpaved Road 700 (Railroad Gulch). Go 3.5 miles to Woodlands Camp, where you need to sign a waiver (see above), then .7 mile farther on Road 730 to the trailhead at the junction with Road 731, just beyond the lily ponds on the right of the road.

FURTHER INFO: Jackson State Forest (707) 964-5674. Mendocino Woodlands Camp (707) 937-5755.

25.

FOREST HISTORY TRAIL

AT THE MENDOCINO WOODLANDS

The sign indicating the start of the trail is 100 feet north of the parking area. The first segment of the trail, which highlights forest ecology, heads northwest on a gentle ascent of Cookhouse Gulch. You pass through forest near the stream, then come to an open meadow at 1/16 mile. About 200 feet beyond you come to a stand of young Douglas fir. While the interpretive brochure points out that Douglas fir does not live as long as redwoods, some live in excess of 750 years.

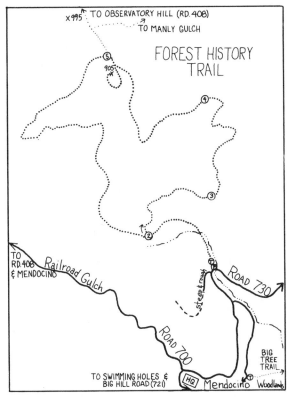

At 1/8 mile you begin to climb above the redwood flood plain of the canyon floor. As you climb a small side stream, notice how many young redwoods are growing on the flat below and the hillsides around you, indicating that this is a prime area for redwood regeneration.

At 1/4 mile you are right alongside the eroded gully of the creek. You soon cross a wooden footbridge, then climb more steeply to marker #12. Your trail then switchbacks right and up onto a steep ridge. As you continue to climb the ridge by switchbacks to 1/2 mile, it becomes more open (#15).

There is a rest bench at 5/8 mile, near the start of the Native American segment of the trail. The next stretch descends slightly then levels through more open forest. After crossing a wooden bridge at 3/4 mile, you climb by rough wooden steps to displays about edible and medicinal plants. One of these is fiddlenecks, the young shoots of bracken fern. Though the author has eaten these and found them quite tasty, it was announced a few years ago that studies showed them to be carcinogenic. Another is

113

poison oak to which the Pomo seem to have had an immunity. Though they ate the berries, do not try it, even if you have some Native American blood.

Just short of one mile you switchback twice, climbing into deep forest. If you are on the trail in summer, you may be able to snack on the huckleberries growing along this stretch of trail.

After another rest bench at the start of the Early Logging History segment of the trail, you climb more steps, cross a small bridge and continue climbing to #25.

The brochure implies that timber cruisers are an extinct breed. Having worked as a timber cruiser until recently, the author is inclined to disagree. They are not, though they are endangered by a surplus of foresters and the stagnant economics of today's logging industry. Also, to say that this tract holds enough lumber for 3 typical three bedroom houses is misleading. There is far too much waste involved in cutting trees less than 2 feet in diameter. It will be at least 50 more years before these trees are really harvestable. Timber cruisers also bore trees, extracting a core sample to determine the age and growth patterns of a tree. From this information it can be estimated when this tract will be large enough to harvest.

The next section of trail climbs steeply to 1 1/8 miles and a bench. After a rest you continue climbing a bit, then drop slightly into another canyon, coming to another bench at 1 3/8 miles. Then climb steeply to #30.

Just below the trail is a small flat where a steam donkey engine was located. This device was invented by a Humboldt County logger about 1880. It quickly replaced the teams of oxen which had been used until then to move logs. Imagine the noise and activity which occurred on this site when the donkey was in operation. (A steam donkey can be seen behind the Guest House Museum in Fort Bragg.)

After passing through a gulch, you climb the steepest hill yet to a rest bench at 1 1/2 miles. Or you can continue climbing a bit farther to another rest bench at the start of the Forest Management segment of your hike.

Your trail continues climbing to 1 5/8 miles from the trailhead where it gains the top of the ridge. Here you will learn the history of reforestation in this area. Though the interpretive brochure states that the Great Depression put an end to reforestation efforts, tree planting is a common practice in modern forestry.

A short downhill stretch of trail is quickly followed by more uphill. Just beyond 1 7/8 miles, a short (1/6 mile) side trail on the left spirals to Observation Point, a 905-foot-high peak with a fine view south and west into the heavily wooded drainage of Big River. Directly below you to the west is Railroad Gulch, the road you drove in on.

Near the bench at the top grows an uncommon tree species, California torreya or nutmeg (no relation to the spice) with dark green pointed needles. Observation Point is the halfway point on this loop hike.

Returning to the junction, your trail heads downhill to a junction with the Manly Gulch trail. Take the left fork and proceed southwest to the start of the Demonstration Forestry segment of the trail. You are walking along a side slope which drops steeply on your right into Railroad Gulch. Watch your step!

At 2 1/4 miles the trail swings to the east. Tanoaks thrive on these rocky slopes. As you begin to descend, you pass a big redwood stump. Notice how well the second growth redwoods are growing in this gully.

You continue descending to 2 1/2 miles just beyond which #43 describes experiments with clones of redwoods. If the word "clone" has a negative connotation, consider that these are merely cuttings taken from the tops of healthy, fast-growing redwoods, just like a gardener might do with roses.

As you continue your descent, a large clearcut area lies below you to the right of the trail. Consider how drastically the clearcut has changed (you might say demolished) the forest environment. Compare it to the healthy second growth forest through which you are walking.

In the next section you may also compare the large clearcut to selective logging (#45) and group selection or small clearcut (#46). These experiments could help to resolve the raging controversy over clearcut versus selective logging.

Just beyond 2 3/4 miles you come to the last item of the intrepretive brochure (#47). The trail goes southeast, then south from here for 1/4 mile to rejoin the main trail at the start of the Native American section of trail. It is one mile downhill to the trailhead.

MONTGOMERY WOODS STATE PARK:

DISTANCE: 1 1/2 miles semi-loop.

TERRAIN: Steep walled canyon with redwood flood plain containing virgin forest.

ELEVATION GAIN/LOSS: 120 feet+/120 feet−

BEST TIME: Spring for wildflowers, summer is good. May be impassable in rainy season.

WARNINGS: Road and trail may be impassable during rainy season. Watch for poison oak along trail. Winding, often narrow road from Highway 1. Drive slowly and carefully.

DIRECTIONS TO TRAILHEAD: Turn east off Highway 1 at M.50.00 onto the Comptche (comp-chee)-Ukiah Road. Go 30 beautiful but winding miles, the last 12 or so alternating paved and gravel surface. Park just east of bridge at M.29.6. OR from Highway 101, exit at M.25.9 just north of Ukiah, taking Orr Springs Road (mostly unpaved) 15 miles west to Montgomery Woods State Park.

FURTHER INFO: Mendocino Area State Parks (707) 937-5804.

26.

MONTGOMERY WOODS STATE PARK
HIGHLAND VIRGIN REDWOOD FOREST

This narrow creek canyon, at the headwaters of Big River, is the most impressive stand of virgin redwoods remaining on public land in Mendocino County. The park, established in 1945 from a seminal donation of 9 acres now comprises 1484 acres, though both trail and virgin redwoods cover only a small center portion. The trail follows Montgomery Creek beneath coastal sempervirens up to 14 feet in diameter, many over 300 feet tall.

An interpretive brochure describes the "climax forest" environment and flora. The brochure is available at the trailhead (April through October).

The main hiking trail starts west of the parking area, heading south up the creek through young redwoods. You quickly come to a small bridge across the creek. Directly across the bridge is a small stand of large redwoods. A side trail leads south into this grove.

The main trail however, is 50 feet beyond, a broad path leading up a steep hill. There is a pit toilet just north of the junction.

Take your time going up this steep incline, as it is the only difficult part of the trail. In a few hundred feet you look down to your left at a small waterfall on the creek. The redwoods here are about five feet in diameter. At 1/8 mile from the car you are still climbing steeply, angling away from the creek. The trail then levels and forks. The main trail goes downhill on the left. (An old trail in the center continues south. The fire road swings to the right and climbs steeply. You can take the latter for an overview of this virgin redwood canyon.)

Take the gentle descent on the left, dropping to a broad redwood flat in the creek canyon. Trilliums and sword ferns abound. Where the trail flattens out you come to redwoods up to 11 feet in diameter. These old giants are about 300 feet tall. This is the Grubb Memorial Grove. If you leave the trail here

step very carefully; tiny calypso orchids bloom from late March to May.

The loop trail begins here. Stay on the right. You soon come to #1 of the guided nature trail, about 1/4 mile from the trailhead. In another 1/16 mile you come to a moss-covered rock ridge, defining the west boundary of the redwood flat. "Five-finger" ferns grow nearby. Poison oak is profuse in this area, both as a bush and as a vine; in the fall, it adorns many of the trees with its yellow and scarlet leaves.

A bit farther, at marker #3, woodwardia ferns grow in a dense thicket to the left of the trail. They grow six or seven feet tall in this protected canyon. Other ferns which grow nearby include licorice, wood, bracken and gold back. You have come 3/8 mile from your car. A redwood growing directly on the left side of the trail has a burl the size of a portable television. When the author walked this trail on Easter '86, the quiet canyon reverberated with a sound like a wooden machine gun; a woodpecker, hidden high above, drilled for bugs in the redwood bark.

Soon you come to marker #4 on your left. A large redwood with a massive fire scar grows by the trail. In their 1000 to 3000 year lives these giants have withstood many major lightning-caused fires, and many more fierce storms and floods. In another 200 feet you pass the MacCallum Grove. Then your trail leads you under a giant fallen redwood, splintered from its jarring fall.

At 1/2 mile the trail follows a small side stream. The grove is more wild and undisturbed on this upper end, away from the heavier foot traffic. Large clumps of ferns and huckleberries thrive here. In between grow redwood sorrel, calypso orchids, false solomon's seal and other shade-loving wildflowers.

In another 100 feet, directly on the left of and leaning toward the trail, a ten-inch-diameter, seven-foot-long redwood branch (or top) has fallen in a storm, wedging itself immovably into the forest floor. The foliage is still green; it appears to have sent down roots from its haphazard "replanting," even though it landed top first. This sprouting is a known redwood characteristic. Though it probably will not survive, in this virgin grove, however, who knows?

The next section of trail follows an old logging "skid" road. The boards in the trail bed were put down so that teams of oxen could drag huge cut logs down the canyon, clear of the often muddy ground. Another 100 feet brings you to the Kellieowen Grove on the right side of the trail. Named to memorialize early Mendocino pioneers (as in the Kelley House in Mendocino village), this grove has smaller trees but is beautifully situated in a small flat side canyon. Redwood benches provide a resting spot.

Just 200 feet after Kellieowen Grove, you can shorten the hike by going left at a sign marked "shorter loop." Our description continues south though, to the right. In about 1/16 mile, you have reached the 5/8 mile point from the trailhead. A giant redwood on the left side of the trail is 13 1/2 feet in diameter, 42 feet in circumference and easily 340 feet tall. The world's tallest known living redwood is 368 feet tall, located in the Tall Trees Grove of Redwood National Park, north of Eureka.

Your trail continues past more ferns, then climbs steps carved into a fallen redwood. You walk on top of this log for about 150 feet. Notice how the redwood flat has built a new level up canyon from this log, burying another six feet of the butts of the redwood giants on your right. Over centuries this process of fallen redwoods forming natural dams has helped create this redwood flat.

At the end of the long fallen-log bridge you have come 3/4 mile. The main trail turns left towards the trailhead. Those more adventuresome can go right, following a trail that becomes vague within an 1/8 mile, leaving the virgin forest for selectively logged, but still large forest. This small trail goes to the headwaters of Montgomery Creek. It is recommended only for people with topo map and compass (and who know how to use them). Near a giant mossy rock clearing on the right side of the canyon, another huge redwood has fallen. The trail picks up again beyond this obstacle but the big trees become sparse.

The trail toward the car: walk northwest on the opposite side of the canyon. Quickly you will see the first Douglas fir intrusion (marker #10) on this virgin redwood forest. Then you duck under another fallen giant. At one mile from the trailhead the track rises above the flat. At 1 1/8 miles, you come to a large moss-covered rock outcrop (#12). At the far end of this is a bench where you can rest.

Soon after you cross two small foot bridges, meeting the shorter loop trail across the creek. Marker #13 is a fine display of upended redwood roots. Glassy, blue-green pools along the creek reflect the ferns and redwoods. At 1 1/4 miles your trail bends to the left across the canyon to rejoin the start of the loop at Grubb Grove. Your car is less than 1/4 mile down the hill.

Before you leave, take a few minutes to wander along the headwaters of the South Fork of Big River. Alders, big leaf maples, and beautiful Pacific dogwoods (bloom in spring) mix with Douglas fir and redwoods along the stream. Bright red Indian warriors and orange California poppies grow in sunny clearings. Think about the time when the whole north coast was dominated by immense virgin redwood groves similiar to the one you just explored.

27

CHAPMAN POINT

SOUTH OF MENDOCINO BAY

This trail leads through sloping, grassy headlands, scattered with Monterey pine and wildflowers, descending to rugged, eroded ocean bluffs. This land was part of the original Beall ranch, settled in the 1850s by one of the earliest pioneer families. The Bealls sold to the Kents in 1857. The Kents later sold to the Spring family, who still own and operate the ranch to the south of this walk. The Springs sold the point to the Chapmans around the turn of the century. The State acquired these 73 acres in 1975. Old maps refer to this area as Chaparral or Mason. The walk is notable for its rugged shoreline, postcard views of Mendocino and wildflowers.

The trail leads due west from the parking area, between a cypress pole fence on the left and a row of planted Monterey pines on the right. You descend gradually toward the shore as postcard views of Mendocino appear on your right. On a clear day, beyond the village loom Point Cabrillo and the rugged mountains of the King Range in the distance.

    The trail wanders through Douglas iris (blooming February to May), then tops a small rise. To the right of the trail is a grassy hilltop. This is a fine blanket picnic spot with a superb view. Beyond here the trail

CHAPMAN POINT:

DISTANCE: 1 1/4 miles semi-loop.

TERRAIN: Gently sloping grassy headlands leading to eroded coastal bluffs.

ELEVATION GAIN/LOSS: 130 feet+/130 feet−

BEST TIME: Spring, but any time is good.

WARNINGS: Watch for killer waves near the bluffs. Stay off adjacent private property. Littering on this pristine land is considered a capital crime.

DIRECTIONS TO TRAILHEAD: 1.6 miles south of Little Lake Road in Mendocino. On west side of Highway 1 at M.48.94. Rough dirt parking opposite Gordon Lane.

FURTHER INFO: Mendocino Area State Parks (707) 937-5804.

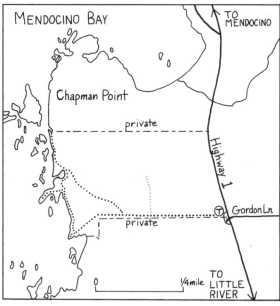

drops steeply from the second to the first marine terrace.

At 1/4 mile your descent eases. Take the left of two forks, still heading west. In less than another 1/4 mile you come to level, open headland. The fence jogs left and so does the trail. The ocean's edge is just beyond.

USE CAUTION HERE: North Coast surf can be dangerous. Watch out for large waves breaking over these low headlands. Furthermore, these eroded cliffs are crumbly and unstable. They consist largely of sand, geologically uplifted from ancient beaches.

Across a small cove to the south, cows and sheep (and occasionally deer) graze contentedly on always fresh green grass. The animals seem oblivious to the crashing surf. Wedged into the sea stacks offshore are the remains of a wrecked fishing boat. Only the mast is visible at high tide.

These headlands offer a fine vantage point to watch for whales, seals, pelicans, cormorants and other sea life. Hawks, kites and many smaller birds live onshore.

The trail north along the headlands clings near the edge of the cliff. In 1/8 mile you come to a point of twisted rock, surrounded by churning surf. The tidal action has worn away the softer rock, creating the hammerhead shape of this point. On a recent visit many harbor seals swam below this point, bobbing in the rough surf. They peered curiously at the humans peering at them.

Continuing north, you wind east around the deeply carved cove north of the point. This cove may be the remains of an ancient blowhole. Just 1/8 mile along the bluff, meet the return trail angling from the southwest.

Before returning however, take a few minutes to walk ahead to the fence marking the northern State Park boundary. Main Street of Mendocino village reappears beyond the fence. Where the fence ends at

bluff's edge, a small natural bridge is visible. Mendocino Bay and the mouth of Big River lie just beyond.

Retrace your steps, returning by the left fork to the top of the hill. Then follow the fence east, back to the parking area.

28.

LITTLE RIVER POINT
PRIME WHALE WATCHING

Like Chapman Point one mile to the north, this grassy headland was part of the original Beall Ranch. This was ranching land, whereas the balance of Little River was devoted almost entirely to logging. The state acquired these 80 acres in 1975, now administered as part of Van Damme State Park.

If you go on this hike, bring your own litter bag. Being totally undeveloped there are no garbage cans and no one will follow along to pick up your mess. PLEASE PACK IT OUT!

The parking lot is on the southwest corner of Highway 1 and unmarked Peterson Lane (named after a pioneer shipbuilder). Walk west on Peterson Lane for 1/8 mile, coming to signs warning "Private Road." Pedestrians do have right of way to the trail. A fence lies where the road turns sharply left. The trail proper starts at the south end of the fence and climbs gently west by northwest over grassy terrain spotted with Monterey pines. About 1/4 mile from the highway, you crest the hill and walk through the trees. Then gradually descending, you see the ocean ahead. It is 1/16 mile to the edge. If the wind blows, you can find some shelter behind the bushy cypresses growing here. Douglas iris bloom in spring. Several different colors of iceplant flowers occur most of the year.

There are flat rocky shelves directly offshore, a favorite haul out for harbor seals. But beyond that it rapidly drops off to a deep channel where migrating whales come very close to shore, giving the whale watcher a great vantage point. You can watch from here or walk north to maximize your view. It is 1/8 mile north along the bluff to the fence on the north boundary of this property. On the way you may have

LITTLE RIVER POINT:

DISTANCE: 1 1/4 to 1 1/2 miles round trip.

TERRAIN: Gently sloping headlands spotted with cypress and Monterey pines leading to rocky shore.

BEST TIME: Any sunny day that is not too windy. High overcast also good. Can be very wet after major rains.

WARNINGS: Stay off private property. On bluffs or tidal rocks, watch for killer waves.

DIRECTIONS TO TRAILHEAD: Park on west side of Highway 1, north end of Little River at M.48.35 (dirt lot just south of Rachel's Inn).

FURTHER INFO: Mendocino Area State Parks (707) 937-5804.

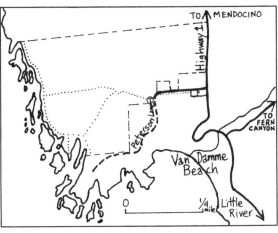

noticed oblong-shaped holes in the dark soil, about 6 inches high and one foot wide. These lead to badger dens. You may take a distant seat and watch for Mr. and Mrs. Badger to emerge, but please do not disturb. (You may have a long wait.)

To the south of the trail you came out on, a narrow footpath wanders along the headland. At 1/16 mile, take the trail which goes east, away from the bluff. In another 1/16 mile, take the right fork. (The trail straight ahead leads east, then south to private property.) You can walk just 250 feet more. You find you are on a promontory which points due south toward an ultramodern home. Brilliant blue iris grow on the wooded end of the point. To your east is a narrow blue lagoon.

Retrace your steps to the cypress and back over the small hill to your car.

29.

VAN DAMME STATE PARK
FERN CANYON TRAIL

This very popular trail is usually crowded with nature lovers during the summer months. My favorite time to visit this deep verdant canyon is in winter or early spring. On a weekday in March, I saw only four other people in the entire length of the canyon. The only negative aspect of winter use is that you must ford the "Little" River 9 times in each direction, a challenging feat at high water.

The trail follows an old skid road used to haul cut redwoods down the canyon by oxen teams from 1864 through 1894.

VAN DAMME STATE PARK:

DISTANCE: 5 miles round trip.

TERRAIN: Gently sloping bottom of deep lush creek canyon. Several fords must be made in winter

ELEVATION GAIN/LOSS: 200 feet+/200 feet−

BEST TIME: Spring to fall.

WARNINGS: Watch for poison oak and stinging nettles along trail. You must ford Little River nine times in each direction. (Fords are paved concrete.)

DIRECTIONS TO TRAILHEAD: Turn off Highway 1 at M.48.05 into Van Damme State Park. Go .5 mile east on the road to the Lower Campground. Off season the trail leaves from campsite #26. In summer the road is open .2 mile farther to signed Fern Canyon trailhead.

FURTHER INFO: Mendocino Area State Parks (707) 937-5804. No-fee parking available on opposite side of Highway 1.

ENVIRONMENTAL CAMPS: Located about 2 miles up the Fern Canyon trail. There are 10 camps in mixed conifer forest near the stream. $6 per night.

OTHER SUGGESTIONS: A 3 1/2 mile loop starts at the end of the paved trail up the canyon. Or you can reach the loop at its top end from the Pygmy Forest trailhead (see below). ELEVATION GAIN/ LOSS: 390 feet+/390 feet−

PYGMY FOREST WALK: A 1/4 mile loop leads through a prime example of pygmy forest. Turn east off Highway 1 at M.47.50, south of Little River. Go 2.85 miles to the signed pygmy forest trailhead on the left. No fee parking available.

The following types of ferns occur in Fern Canyon: western sword, bracken, deer, five-finger, lady, licorice, horsetail, wood, bird's foot, and occasional gold back (or stamp) ferns.

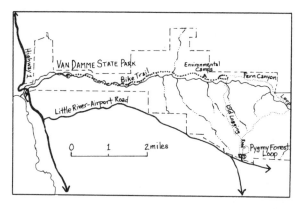

Starting at campsite #26 (can start farther east in summer), head east on the paved road for 1/8 mile to the first stream crossing. In winter or spring you should use this ford as a bellwether to gauge how difficult all of the crossings upstream are. If you have trouble crossing here, it will be no better ahead.

Ferns grow nearly everywhere in the canyon: both north- and south-facing slopes, on trees and stumps, and out of rocks. Other common species in the understory below second growth redwoods, firs and hemlocks include redwood sorrel, salal, coastal man-root, stinging nettle, columbine, and elder-, thimble-, red huckle- and rasp-berries.

You come to the second ford about 3/4 mile from the trailhead. The third is just beyond. After the fourth ford, five-finger, sword and lady ferns grow right next to the trail. Uphill by a tiny waterfall on the right grows wild ginger. In 500 feet, pig-a-back plant grows in the shade to the right of the trail.

Continue up the canyon, crossing Little River at the fifth, sixth and seventh fords up to the 1 1/4-mile point. Beyond the seventh ford the canyon broadens.

After crossing the stream for the eighth time, at 1 3/4 miles you come to the first of ten pleasant environmental (walk or bicycle-in) camps. This is a quiet, pristine spot, a real treat for anyone who has been riding their bike along busy Highway 1.

At 2 1/4 miles the road forks into a small loop. It is 1/4 mile before the paved road ends.

At the end of the loop, two dirt trails lead off in different directions. They form a more arduous 3 1/2-mile loop. (See OTHER SUGGESTION.)

Return down the canyon to your starting point.

30

NAVARRO-BY-THE-SEA

SWEEPING VIEWS FROM THE OLD HIGHWAY

This short trail climbs to and follows the old coast highway to spectacular views of Navarro River mouth and surroundings.

From the unimproved parking area, the trail heads east, then northeast. You rapidly begin to climb the steep hill as the trail switchbacks through dense vegetation. The trail winds around a lone cypress.

About 1/10 mile you come to the pavement of the old highway. From here you have a grand view of the Navarro River mouth and beach. Offshore are several sea stacks including the Arch of the Navarro. Harbor seals can often be seen in the river near the mouth. In winter they come to gorge themselves on the salmon and steelhead which have come to spawn upriver. The seals feast playfully as seagulls chase after them for fish scraps.

Turning right on the pavement, you climb gradually along the bluff. The asphalt is rapidly becoming overgrown by the tangle of vegetation which surrounds it. Dominant species include ceanothus, lupine, Douglas iris, blackberries, and sticky monkeyflower.

Soon you come to a fallen rusted old guardrail. Where the road surface has been eroded you can see

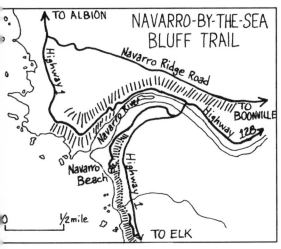

NAVARRO-BY-THE-SEA
BLUFF TRAIL

TO ALBION

Highway 1

Navarro Ridge Road

Navarro River

TO BOONVILLE

Highway 128

Navarro Beach

Highway 1

TO ELK

½ mile

NAVARRO-BY-THE-SEA:

DISTANCE: 1 mile round trip.

TERRAIN: Old road across steep, brushy headlands with commanding views of ocean and river mouth.

ELEVATION GAIN/LOSS: 200 feet+/200 feet−

BEST TIME: Anytime.

WARNINGS: Watch for poison oak as you climb the trail.

DIRECTIONS TO TRAILHEAD: On Highway 1 just south of the Highway 128 junction and the Navarro River bridge, turn west at M.40.15. Go .75 mile to signed Navarro Bluff trailhead.

FURTHER INFO: CalTrans (707) 445-6423 (Eureka).

OTHER SUGGESTIONS: A walk along the broad NAVARRO BEACH is an easy alternative to climbing the bluffs, though in summer it is often packed with campers. If you go in winter be sure to watch for killer waves.

There are many swimming holes along the NAVARRO RIVER southeast of here, accessed by Highway 128.

Especially for mountain bikers and equestrians, NAVARRO RIDGE ROAD is a county road which runs along the ridge north of the river. The 13.35 mile road has very light traffic on its easternmost 8 miles. It is unpaved for the eastern 10 miles. Access is at M.11.60 on Highway 128 on the east end and at M.40.35 on Highway 1 on the west end. Watch and listen for gunfire; avoid in hunting season.

the old redwood supports of the road. Just beyond, a mudslide, now overgrown with vegetation, covers the pavement. Uphill a stunted grand fir grows. A few paces up the road, an old turnout provides views south to Point Arena on a clear day.

At 1/4 mile from the trailhead, you come to another large mud slide. In another 200 feet, mud changes abruptly to bedrock. Watch for falling rocks here, especially in wet weather. Above you a house sits precariously at the top of the rock slide.

You soon pass a stand of windblown cypress on the steep slope below you. On the uphill side, wild red columbine and sticky monkeyflower bloom nearly year round. At a major sinking of the old roadbed the trail veers right and drops 5 feet. Though this sloughing looks rather unstable, it is not likely to slide away under your feet.

A bit farther you cross a small stream (dry in summer) nearly at the top of the bluff. Just beyond, 3/8 mile from your starting point, the road reaches still-maintained pavement and a sign, the back of which warns "Road closed because of storm damage and slides." A small cluster of houses lies just beyond.

Here you have climbed to an elevation of about 160 feet. Looking west from here, you can see where the water changes from milky blue-green to a deep blue, indicating deep water. Looking back from where you have come, you see a bird's-eye view of the beach, river mouth and the 600-foot rise of the steep headlands beyond the Navarro River. When you have had your fill of the view, return by the same path.

If you are not ready to return to your car, you can walk north from where the trail drops to the beach. The trail goes about 1/10 mile before coming to a fence marking private property. Please do not go beyond this point. Notice how the environment changes to an entirely different shady riparian habitat. Here stinging nettles, red alders, sword ferns and thimbleberries thrive in the cool shade of the north-facing hillside. Moss and lichen even grow directly on the old road surface, helping to return it to a more natural state.

HENDY WOODS STATE PARK

Though there are other trailheads in the Park, all trail descriptions in this guide originate from the picnic area by the river.

Hendy Woods represents the only link to what Anderson Valley was like before logging began around 1860. About 100 acres of the Park's 650 acres are virgin forest. The climate of the valley is warmer and drier than it was when the first white settlers arrived. This has occurred for the same reason that your walk in the redwoods is cooler than the sunny picnic area.

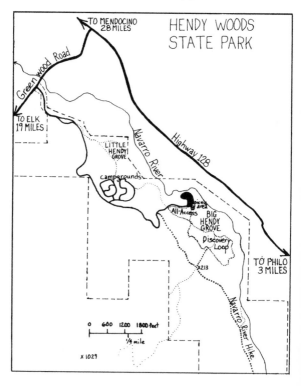

31.

GENTLE GIANTS LOOP

ALL ACCESS TRAIL

Go south from the parking area toward the tall redwoods, quickly entering the relatively cool shade of the forest. Soon there is a wooden trail map and a box where you can get a brochure for the nature trail. Just

GENTLE GIANTS LOOP:

DISTANCE: 3/8 mile loop or 1/2 mile round trip.
TERRAIN: Flat virgin redwood forest.
BEST TIME: April through October.
WARNINGS: Watch for traffic on paved road.
DIRECTIONS TO TRAILHEAD: Leave Highway 1 at M.40.08. Go south on 128 to M.20.15 where you turn right. Go .5 mile to State Park entrance on the left. Follow this road to the picnic area at its end, 1.8 miles. (Note: Highway 128 runs from Highway 101 at Cloverdale northwest to Highway 1 at the Navarro River mouth — about 10 miles south of Mendocino.)
FURTHER INFO: Mendocino Area State Parks (707) 937-5804.

beyond on the left is a tree finder device which points out some common hardwood species. In another 100 feet you enter even cooler virgin redwood forest. The redwoods here have diameters to 8 or 9 feet and range to 270 feet tall. Just beyond a scarred giant at 1/8 mile from your starting point, you come to a small bridge. The trail continues through deep forest where little sunlight penetrates. Soon you come to a junction; the Discovery trail is on your left. Gentle Giant continues on the right, quickly coming to a huge fire scarred redwood with an oblong base. The narrow side is "only" 12 feet, the longer side nearly 17 feet! You soon cross another small bridge passing many giants, all fire scarred. In 1/4 mile from its start the trail crosses one more very small bridge and shortly comes to the road. You can return the way you came or, with caution, turn right and go downhill on the road shoulder 1/8 mile to your car.

```
┌─────────────────────────────────────────┐
│          DISCOVERY LOOP:                  │
├─────────────────────────────────────────┤
│                                           │
│ DISTANCE: 3/4 mile loop (You can add the 5/8 │
│    mile outer loop or the remote trail if you want a │
│    longer hike.)                          │
│ TERRAIN: Flat, virgin redwood forest.     │
│ BEST TIME: April through October. Though trail │
│    may be wet in winter, it is still a fine walk with │
│    proper footwear.                       │
│ WARNINGS: Watch for poison oak growing near the │
│    trail.                                 │
│ DIRECTIONS TO TRAILHEAD: Same as #31.     │
│ FURTHER INFO: Mendocino Area State Parks  │
│    (707) 937-5804.                        │
│                                           │
└─────────────────────────────────────────┘
```

32.

DISCOVERY LOOP
THROUGH GIANT REDWOODS

Follow the Gentle Giant trail from the parking area
for about 1/8 mile. Near a wooden bridge, take the
left fork. In about 200 feet you come to the root end
of a huge fallen redwood tree, #5 in the interpretive
brochure. You are on a flat river flood plain, a prime
habitat for redwoods.

In 1/4 mile from the parking lot you come to a
forest clearing at the edge of the flood plain (#6).
The rise in front of you is the ancient riverbank. In
100 feet you come to a loveseat cut from a chunk of
redwood on the left of the trail. The next section of
trail is slippery after rains (watch your step). On this
part of the flood plain, a small creek fans out to
deposit silt and keep the forest floor moist. Notice
that the redwood giants seem to especially love it
here.

You soon come to a memorial bench and grove, a

fine place to sit and listen to the quiet of this place. The uncommon woodwardia fern joins sword and bracken ferns along the next section of trail. Near 3/8 mile the trail curves around a fallen giant. This tree left a 75-foot-high splinter when it fell.

In another 75 feet the trail comes to a main junction. The signs are confusing. For the continuation of the Discovery trail, go left here. The Outer Loop trail straight ahead takes you on a longer tour of the grove. You may take the Outer Loop without missing any of the Discovery loop. Add an extra 5/8 mile to the total distance. On the right, the trail marked with a sign "FIRE ROAD" leads to the Navarro River hike.

The Discovery trail continues northeast. Many green leafy plants grow on the forest floor: redwood sorrel, Pacific vanilla leaf (3 lobe-shaped leaves), salal, huckleberry and sword and bracken ferns. Just 250 feet from the junction, the Outer Loop rejoins the Discovery Loop. Your trail turns left here (A horse trail leads out of the grove and to a corral near the river.) You pass an old stump, evidence of the logging that occurred on the fringes of Big Hendy Grove before it became a state park in 1958. About 1/2 mile from your starting point you pass under a low bridge of fallen redwood logs and a living bay laurel. Just beyond, at #15, you can examine a redwood burl.

In another 200 feet, you come to a rest bench and #16. A redwood giant hangs over your head, leaning at a seemingly precarious angle. Redwoods have the ability to buttress themselves however. When a redwood starts to lean, it puts on extra growth beneath the lean, counteracting the tendency to fall.

In another 200 feet, your trail returns to the early part of the loop (near #5). Turn right and you will be back at the parking and picnic area where you started.

33.

NAVARRO RIVER HIKE
THROUGH THE HENDY BACKWOODS

At the junction on the Discovery trail, take the right fork. From the redwood flat, you start climbing alongside a small mossy drainage. In 1/8 mile the trail levels out and comes to a gravel fire road. The

NAVARRO RIVER HIKE:

DISTANCE: 3 miles round trip.

TERRAIN: Virgin redwood forest leading to a gravel fire road along the Navarro River.

BEST TIME: April through October.

WARNINGS: Watch for poison oak.

DIRECTIONS TO TRAILHEAD: Follow directions in #31 to picnic area. Walk the Gentle Giant trail to the Discovery trail. The river trail branches right from the halfway point of the Discovery trail.

FURTHER INFO: Mendocino Area State Parks (707) 937-5804.

gravel road immediately forks into two roads (trails for the purpose of this report). The main trail is on the left.

(You can take the right fork to extend the hike or as an alternate. Go uphill 1/8 mile to a fork in the road. Take the left fork. In another 200 feet, go left again, quickly crossing a small creek and continuing uphill. You soon must climb over a large fallen log. About 1/6 mile beyond you come to the State Park boundary. Though the trail, actually an old logging road, continues uphill, this is private property.)

You are 1/2 mile from the picnic area. Taking the left fork of the fire road, your mostly level trail heads southeast. At 5/8 mile the trail bends to the right and heads up a slight hill. A little farther you cross a small stream; redwoods to 7 feet in diameter grow alongside. At 7/8 mile you pass a sign indicating a horse trail on the left, but your route continues on the gravel road. (The horse trail leads to the river and follows the river bed back to the picnic area). At one mile from the trailhead the road has climbed above the forest floor on your left. Notice how different the forest floor is here than back in the virgin redwood forest. This is a natural, undisturbed mixed conifer/hardwood forest, not trampled by thousands of state park visitors each year.

About 1 1/4 miles from the trailhead, the terrain

to the left of your path steepens. You may be able to hear the Navarro River below you. In 1/16 mile another horse trail leads toward the river. Stay on the road, crossing another small creek. At 1 7/16 miles the river is directly below you, about 60 feet down the hill. Just beyond, at 1 1/2 miles, you come to the State Park boundary and your turnaround point. From here the town of Philo is just about one mile southeast, but it is all private property in between.

Return along the same route by which you came.

34.

GREENWOOD STATE BEACH

CLIFFS AND SEA STACKS

The present town of Elk was first settled in the 1850s as Greenwood. One of the first settlers was Caleb Greenwood, whose father was an organizer of the ill-fated Donner party. In fact Caleb organized one of the expeditions which went to Donner Lake to save the survivors from their winter of horror. One of the many doghole ports along the Mendocino Coast, Greenwood outlasted other nearby boom towns like Cuffeys Cove

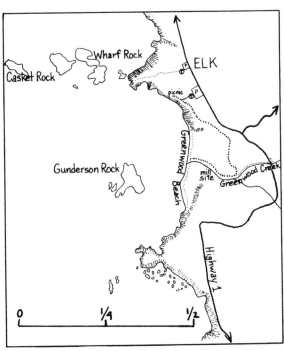

GREENWOOD STATE BEACH:

DISTANCE: 3/4 to 1 1/2 mile round trip.

TERRAIN: From coastal bluff down to beach in a protected cove at the mouth of Greenwood Creek. Sea stacks offshore.

ELEVATION LOSS/GAIN: 150 feet+/150 feet −

BEST TIME: Anytime.

WARNINGS: Trail to beach is an easement across private property; please do not disturb occupants of adjacent houses. Never turn your back on the ocean. Always watch out for rogue waves, especially in winter.

DIRECTIONS TO TRAILHEAD: In the town of Elk, 15 1/2 miles south of Mendocino, parking is on west side of Highway 1 at M.34.05, opposite the Elk Store.

FURTHER INFO: Mendocino Area State Parks (707) 937-5804.

OTHER SUGGESTION: Another short trail leaves from north of post office at M.34.15 heading due west over a high flat bluff to a narrow point with a windblown cypress. On the north side of the point, you can see the remnants of an old loading chute on the rocks below.

to the north and Elk River, Bridgeport, and Alder Creek to the south.

Until ten years ago, the sleepy town of Elk was one of the Mendocino Coast's best kept secrets. Now the existence of several fine inns and a couple of restaurants has brought Elk a bit of new found acclaim. But please try not to tell the whole world about it.

The trail leaves from the graveled parking lot opposite the Elk Store. (There are several picnic tables and a toilet just west of the parking lot for those not willing or able to make the hike down to the beach.) In about

150 feet the main trail to the beach goes left, while a fork to the right leads in another 250 feet to a fine picnic area with an expansive view of the beach below.

The main trail continues downhill just below several private residences, then follows an old drainage ditch to the bottom of the hill, about 1/4 mile. Here another picnic area is located on a flat, the site of one of Greenwood's lumber mills. Another restroom is nearby. A trail from the east meets the main trail near the picnic area. This leads upstream along Greenwood Creek and back to the Highway, providing access to the creek for steelhead fishermen. Wild nasturtiums grow near the junction.

Walk west from the picnic area, coming to a large pile of driftwood marking the extreme high tide line. To the south across the creek, you can make out the remains of the spillway to an old dam, the lake of which was used to hold the logs before cutting at the mill. Continue another 300 feet to the midpoint of the beach. From this point you can walk north or south along the beach.

Just offshore are several large sea stacks with wave tunnels. The one to the left is Gunderson Rock. To the right are Wharf Rock, with the flat top where a loading wharf was once anchored, and Casket Rock. Looking farther to sea between the latter two rocks, you can see Cove Rock, just south of jutting Cuffeys Point. Cove Rock was used by early navigators to locate Greenwood and Cuffeys Coves and safely steer their ships into anchor.

From the center point of the beach, you can walk about 1/8 mile south to the mouth of the creek. The beach continues for a few hundred feet beyond the mouth before coming to a cliff. To the north you may walk nearly 1/4 mile before you come to an impassable cliff.

Return up the hill by the trail upon which you descended.

35

MANCHESTER STATE BEACH
GENTLE BUT WILD COAST

*The hike is described from the north end, starting at
Alder Creek, where the San Andreas Fault leaves the
land and heads north into the ocean. However, you
may start at any one of the four access points. The long
beach curves across prevailing ocean currents, forming
a catch basin for sea debris, a beachcomber's paradise.*

A triangular lagoon sits at the mouth of Alder Creek.
(The beach continues north of the lagoon for 1 1/4
miles to Irish Gulch, ending at impassable cliffs 1/4
mile beyond Irish Beach.) Walk west at the base of
cliffs covered with wildflowers. At 1/16 mile, a suc-
culent garden grows on the cliff. Short of 1/8 mile you
come out on the broad, driftwood-strewn beach. Head
south toward Point Arena lighthouse.

At 1/4 mile the cliffs behind the beach are covered
with sea grass, which has escaped from the dunes just
south of here. At 1/2 mile the cliffs have ended;
grass-covered dunes lie behind the beach. In another
1/16 mile a small gully runs through the dunes. (If you
walk up the gully, you will come to the walk-in environmental camps.

Continuing south along the beach, at 5/8 mile you
come to the broad outflow of Davis Lake. The narrow
lagoon is 200 feet east of the beach. (You can also get
to the environmental camps by turning east here.)
Walking south, the driftwood-strewn beach is backed
by more dunes. The dunes become quite high at about
one mile.

At 1 1/8 miles you come to a path leading out of the
dunes from the main parking area at the end of Kinney
Road. The beach becomes even broader here as you
continue south. The dunes are soon replaced by wild-
flower-covered bluffs. A bright yellow sign proclaims
"CABLE LANDING"; this is where the trans-Pacific
cable heads west.

At 1 5/8 miles from the Alder Creek trailhead, you
come to the mouth of Brush Creek. At 1 3/4 miles, to
the east of the beach lies a lagoon strewn with large
redwood driftwood. Though the lagoon is small, it

MANCHESTER STATE BEACH:

DISTANCE: 3 3/4 miles one way, Alder Creek to Garcia River mouth. 5 miles one way, Irish Beach to Garcia River mouth or any portion of this as a shorter round trip.

TERRAIN: Long beach backed by coastal dunes and cliffs with lagoons, creeks and river mouth.

BEST TIME: Spring and fall. In summer, area is subject to high winds.

WARNINGS: Do not trespass on adjacent private land. Off-road vehicles are not allowed on the dunes. Fires permitted only in fire rings. Watch for rogue waves when on the beach.

DIRECTIONS TO TRAILHEAD: West of Highway 1 near Manchester, several access roads lead west to the park:

Alder Creek at M.22.48, go .7 mile to end of road.

Kinney Road at M.21.40, go .7 mile, then right for Environmental Camp parking. Just over 1 mile to main beach parking at end of road.

Stoneboro Road at M.19.65, go 1.6 miles to end of road. Trail leads west.

Miners Hole Road at M.17.55 for Garcia River access, 1.25 miles from highway.

FURTHER INFO: Mendocino Area State Parks (707) 937-5804.

ENVIRONMENTAL CAMPS: Located near Davis Lake, 10 pleasant environmental camps are accessible from a trail which leaves from the parking area at .7 mile on Kinney Road. Camps are $3/night. It is approximately 1 mile from the trailhead to the environmental camps. The trail leads north, then west past a pond, then turns north along the west shore of Davis Lake. The campsites are just north of the lake, located in coastal dunes and along a cypress windbreak.

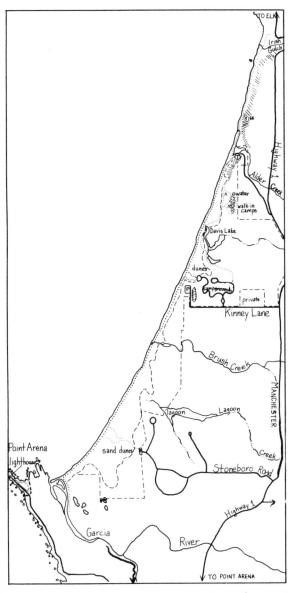

marks the start of a broad wild area that is home to
birds and other wildlife. (In earlier days, Brush Creek
was infamous for its large population of bears.)

The beach continues southwest, the Point Arena
lighthouse looming ever larger. At 2 miles, more
dunes lie to the east. At 2 1/4 miles, large Hunter's
Lagoon hides in the dunes 1/4 mile east. Though only
the west end of the lagoon lies within Park boundaries,
the mile-long, landlocked lake is a fine bird habitat.
Climb the sand hills if you would like a better look.

The long beach continues south, now backed by dunes up to 80 feet in elevation. At 2 3/4 miles you meet several trails from the east. These lead through the dunes to the parking area at the end of Stoneboro Road.

Approximately 3 1/4 miles from Alder Creek, the dunes become narrower and lower. At 3 3/4 miles, you arrive at the narrow sand spit at the mouth of the Garcia River. The lighthouse lies less than 1/4 mile to the west, across the broad river mouth. Even if you were to ford the river, private agricultural lands prevent you from hiking to the lighthouse (see trail #36).

Unless you have arranged a shuttle, you have no choice but to return the way you came.

36.

POINT ARENA LIGHTHOUSE & HEADLANDS
CLIMB TO VIEWS AND HISTORY

This is not a trail per se, *but rather a climb to the top of a 115 foot lighthouse with a fine view and a fascinating history. Though the climb is short compared to other "trails" in this book, it will certainly get your blood pumping and relieve the road blues, if you are traveling far that day. In the spring, a short walk around the grounds of the lighthouse provides access to a wonderful variety of wildflowers and great views up and down the coast.*

The Point Arena lighthouse was established in 1870 at one of the most treacherous sections of the Mendocino Coast for ship traffic. Operated by the U.S. Lighthouse Service, the original oil lamp was visible for 18 miles or more.

The original tower stood slightly shorter than the one in place today. The same earthquake which devastated San Francisco in 1906 shook, swayed, and finally cracked the original brick tower. Though it was the only brick building in Point Arena which was still standing after the quake, it was severely damaged.

The Lighthouse Service razed the structure and built the current tower, the first earthquake resistant, steel reinforced concrete lighthouse in the United

POINT ARENA LIGHTHOUSE & HEADLANDS:

DISTANCE: 145 steps to top of lighthouse (equivalent to 6-8 story building; it is 115 feet high). Also an optional headlands loop of 1/2 mile.

TERRAIN: Flat coastal headlands at end of long point. Steep stairs to top of lighthouse.

BEST TIME: A clear day. The headlands are best in spring when the wildflowers are at their peak — April, May best. February, March and June next best.

WARNINGS: Lighthouse is open 362 days a year from 11 a.m. to 2:30 p.m. Closed Thanksgiving, Christmas and New Year's Days. Lighthouse is also closed during extremely high winds or ferocious storms.

DIRECTIONS TO TRAILHEAD: Turn west off Highway 1 just north of Point Arena at M.17.05. Go 2.7 miles on bumpy but paved and scenic Lighthouse Road.

FEES: $2 for adults, $.50 for children.

FURTHER INFO: Point Arena Lighthouse Keepers (707) 882-2777.

States. It was later turned over to the Coast Guard.

After more than 100 years of human operation, the lighthouse was automated in 1977, putting an end to public access, as the Coast Guard staff was reduced, then eliminated. Local citizens formed a non-profit organization to reopen the historic lighthouse to the public. In 1984 they received a 25 year renewable lease allowing them to open the tower to public tours. The group has established a small museum in the pre-earthquake Fog Signal Building. The fine little museum includes old foghorns, uniforms, flags and historic photographs of the lighthouse, earthquake damage, nearby shipwrecks, and other local history. They also have a great map collection and an exhibit of native flowers.

Pay your admission at the museum before entering the lighthouse.

As you enter the tower at its base, notice a brass plaque set in the first step. The cast iron steps were made in San Francisco in 1869. A sign warns that the 145 steps to the top are equivalent to a six-story building. Take your time as you climb the spiral staircase. Glass brick windows allow an occasional glimpse of the headlands and sea cliffs below you.

At step #145, you come to a landing where you will meet the tour guide. The center of the room is filled by cylindrical machinery, the center shaft of which held the original lamp. Looking up you will see the incredible Fresnel (pron. frānel) lens. This two-ton, glass and brass lens was made in Paris (by the original Fresnel factory) in 1870, shipped around Cape Horn in pieces and assembled here, probably by a company representative sent with it. The two-ton apparatus was precisely engineered to magnify the intensity of the original oil lamp into a beam which carried 18 miles out to sea (the current high-tech light is only rated to carry 25 miles!) The lamp rests on a mercury bath, strong enough to hold the weight yet fluid enough that the massive lens could be turned by a 1/8 horsepower motor.

At this level of the light tower you can look out a small door to the point and the rocky shoals beyond, site of many shipwrecks over the years. You can then go up about 8 steep steps to the very top of the tower where the lens is located. A canvas curtain over the windows keeps direct sunlight off the lens; even a few seconds of direct sun on the powerful lens could start a fire. You may look behind the curtain at the wonderful view but be sure to keep the curtain between you and the lens. Do not touch the lens please, as the lighthouse keepers must keep it clean.

Descend the tower, perhaps reflecting on the marvels of engineering in the nineteenth century.

If you would like to walk more before leaving, a short loop leads east behind the vacation rental homes on an old road track. It is about 1/2 mile around the flower-studded headlands behind the homes, returning along the main road.

37.

SCHOONER GULCH

BOWLING BALL BEACH

The State acquired this 53 acre jewel of a beach for the State Park system in 1985. It is the southernmost holding of the Mendocino Area State Parks. As of May, 1986, there was still a NO TRESPASSING *sign posted at the trailhead. You have been so good about not trespassing up to now that you get to ignore the sign here.*

The trail heads west into a tiny stand of redwoods, then turns south and drops towards the creek. You pass gnarled, burned-out redwood stumps which have healthy young sprouts. After 200 feet the habitat changes to lush riparian. Thimble- and salmonberries grow in a dense thicket along the creek, intertwined with beach pea and other moisture loving plants. If the day is windy, you will find that the little canyon affords protection from the gusts.

About 1/10 mile from your starting point you come to a fork in the trail. The right fork leads up onto the headlands for wildflowers and fine views. Take the left fork which leads to the blond beach in about 200 feet. As you ford the creek over driftwood logs, you

SCHOONER GULCH:

DISTANCE: 1/4 to 2 miles round trip, depending on tide.

TERRAIN: Along verdant creek to its mouth at protected pocket cove. At low tide, beach extends south along cliffs and north through a wave tunnel to a separate beach.

BEST TIME: Low tide, but main beach accessible even at high tide. Spring best for wildflowers, summer for berries.

WARNINGS: Do not get trapped by rising tide if you go north or south from main beach. Always watch the ocean for rogue waves.

DIRECTIONS TO TRAILHEAD: Parking is on west side of Highway 1 at M.11.4, opposite Schooner Gulch Road.

FURTHER INFO: Mendocino Area State Parks (707) 937-5804.

come to the beach of fine sand scattered with rounded, eroded rocks, the "bowling balls" in the popular name. If the tide is high you will not be able to get far to the south, while the north will be impassable.

The trail description continues as if you are there at a minus tide. *Do not attempt the rest of the trail if the tide is higher, or if it has turned and is rising.*

GOING SOUTH: The wide part of the beach extends about 1/16 mile. From there the sand strip quickly narrows, then ends, with cliffs on your left and algae-covered, eroded rocks on your right. From there you must use caution on the slippery rocks. It is an easy scramble over the rocks to a flat, eroded shelf of sandstone, the "bowling lanes" of Bowling Ball Beach. This point is about 1/8 mile from the creek. Walk the smooth, slippery shelf for another 250 feet to its end. From there a jumble of tidal rocks extends about 1/4 mile south to a sandy point. Extensive tide pools lie on your right, home to many varieties of seaweed, a few crabs, snails and anemones. *If the tide is low enough* you may be able to continue around the sandy point.

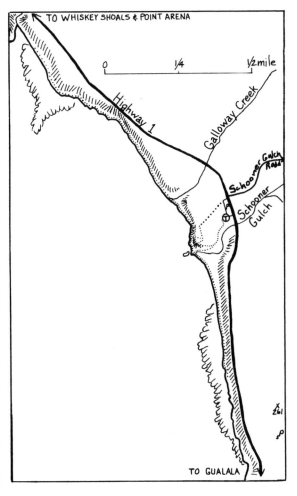

TO WHISKEY SHOALS & POINT ARENA

0   1/4   1/2 mile

Highway 1

Galloway Creek

Schooner Gulch Road

Schooner Gulch

261

TO GUALALA

GOING NORTH FROM THE CREEK: The beach extends about 300 feet, though you must again ford the creek. Here you encounter a wave tunnel, eroded from large, stratified, diagonal blocks of sandstone. You can peer through the tunnel to the cliffs and beach of Whiskey Shoals beyond. If you are sure the tide is not rising, you may continue.

Entering the tunnel, you come to a window after 50 feet. This looks out toward the cliffs of Whiskey Shoals to the northwest. Beyond the window the tunnel becomes more narrow, wet, and slippery. Be careful. Goose neck barnacles grow on the walls. In another 100 feet you emerge onto tidal rocks at the far end of the tunnel. In 200 feet the tidal zone broadens to a rocky beach. In another 200 feet you climb over a rocky ledge to a long, narrow beach with extensive tidal rocks offshore. This beach extends for nearly a mile at low tide, joining the Whiskey Shoals property at the far end.

Returning to the mouth of the creek, it is an easy 1/8 mile uphill to your car.

37A.

WHISKEY SHOALS
CLOSED UNTIL FURTHER NOTICE

Coastal access at Whiskey Shoals/Moat Creek is officially closed as of publication time. The property west of Highway 1 between M.13.08 on the north and M.12.70 on the south has been used for years by divers, fishermen and other locals. The property was managed by the the nonprofit California Institute of Environmental Studies until 1985. When CIES turned the management of Whiskey Shoals over to a local organization, that group could not afford the several fold increase in liability insurance, a result of the "deep pocket" insurance problems. So Whiskey Shoals, a traditional coastal access point, became a victim of the insurance industry's bottom line.

The General Services Administration of the State of California now manages the property, while the State Coastal Conservancy holds the deed. Those agencies are not allowed to provide public access, but they can lease the property to a nonprofit group for that purpose.

The State hopes to develop the beautiful blufftops at Whiskey Shoals as a low density subdivision, which would facilitate development of recreational facilities there. The State acquired the land after a much higher density development failed to materialize. Whatever else happens, it is essential that the State preserve and reopen the beautiful cliffs and beaches at Whiskey Shoals for public use.

Before the recent problems arose, plans were underway to develop a five-mile coastal blufftop trail running through the Whiskey Shoals property and south to Schooner Gulch. State legislation and the newly adopted Mendocino County Local Coastal Plan both promote the development of this trail. But nothing can proceed until the insurance fiasco is resolved.

By the way, the name Whiskey Shoals harkens back

to the days of prohibition, when these isolated shores, hidden by their steep cliffs, were a popular spot for rum runners to land their illegal cargo.

GUALALA POINT
REGIONAL PARK

The park is in a spectacular setting on the south shore of the normally placid Gualala River, extending upstream from its mouth for about 1 1/2 miles. The land was the northernmost portion of the Rancho German land grant, donated to Sonoma County when Oceanic Properties created the extensive subdivision called Sea Ranch. The park covers the diverse habitats of beach, rugged sea cliffs, grassy headlands, tidal river and redwood and bay laurel forests. It is just across the Mendocino County line, at the extreme northwest corner of Sonoma County.

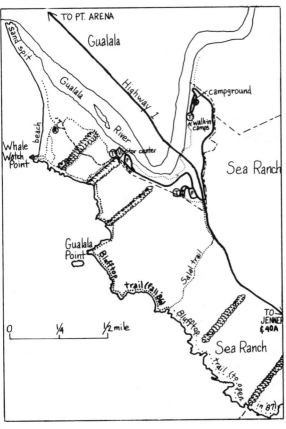

DISTANCE: 1 1/4 mile loop.

TERRAIN: Grassy headlands between river and sea cliffs leading to broad beach at river mouth, then to rocky point.

BEST TIME: Spring is best for wildflowers, whale watching is best December through March. Anytime is good.

WARNINGS: Watch for poison oak tangled with other plants. Private property to south of park; please do not cross fence. Watch for killer waves on beach: six people were swept into the sea here in February 1986; one of them drowned.

DIRECTIONS TO TRAILHEAD: Turn west off Highway 1 at M.58.2 (Sonoma County), about .25 mile south of the town of Gualala. Drive .5 mile to the Visitors Center. The trail starts there.

FURTHER INFO: Gualala Point Regional Park (707) 785-2377.

38.

HEADLANDS to BEACH LOOP
WINDBREAKS AND WILDFLOWERS

The western portion of the park is covered by a fine network of trails which offer several choices. Though the following trail report details the unpaved headlands-to-beach loop, a paved bicycle and wheelchair path can easily be followed out to the same beach and headlands area.

The modern visitor center fits nicely into the beautiful headlands landscape. It is powered by a wind generator standing just north of the building. The center has informative displays and provides a welcome refuge from the strong winds which often blow here.

From the visitor center, follow the paved path northwest for 200 feet. There you meet a grassy trail which continues northwest where the paved path swings west. Take the grassy path leading gently downhill through lush headlands. In 1/16 mile a trail on your right heads downhill to a nice picnic area near the river.

Continuing northwest, in 100 feet you meet another trail, on your left this time, which leads southwest on the leeward side of a cypress windbreak to another picnic area. The main trail continues west by northwest around the old windbreak, passing through grassy headlands filled with wildflowers.

On your right the Gualala River is a prime habitat for aquatic birds. Near the trail live many species of grasslands birds.

About 1/4 mile from the trailhead the footpath joins the paved trail, continuing to the beach near the river mouth. In late summer or early fall you can ford the river near its mouth, continuing north to the end of the beach. At medium to high water, however, the river is not safe to ford.

Our trail description turns southwest on a fork of the paved path, quickly coming to a restroom and to the end of the paved path in about 300 feet. The grassy path continues south from here, following the edge of the bluff overlooking the beach.

The trail forks again in another 200 feet. Here you can choose either the left path, protected behind a row of cypress, or the right fork, continuing along the spectacularly eroded sandstone bluffs above the beach.

At 3/16 mile from the restroom (not quite 1/2 mile from your trailhead), bear right into a "tunnel" through the cypress trees. Here your trail heads west onto a narrow rocky promontory known as Whale Watch Point. It soon comes to sandy bluffs on the leeward side of a cypress windbreak, overlooking ocean cliffs on the south. You may continue 250 feet farther west to the windswept point beyond the windbreak. From here you look north for a fine view of the beach and the town of Gualala. The wooded ridge beyond extends west to the point of Haven's Neck and the big sea stack called Fish Rock.

Returning to the sandy bluff east of the cypress trees, take the right fork southwest along the bluff's edge. You quickly come to a stairway on your right which leads to a flat, rocky tidal shelf (fishing access). Continuing along the bluff you soon plunge into a broad cypress windbreak, a home for many small birds. As you clear the cypress thicket, you meet the windbreak trail forking to the left. (You may return by that trail if you prefer.)

The trail continues southeast near the edge of the bluff. Two benches along this stretch provide resting places with fine views of the coast. In 1/16 mile after the second bench you come to a fence and a sign indicating the park boundary. The start of the new Blufftop trail leads through the fence here (see trail #40). You turn northeast here following the fence and windbreak along the Sea Ranch boundary. In another 1/16 mile you enter a "tunnel" through pines. Leaving the tunnel you meet the paved path in 200 feet. Follow the bike path for the final 1/10 mile back to the visitor center and your car.

39

RIVER TRAIL SOUTH
ALONG A QUIET STEELHEAD STREAM

The campground along the Gualala River lies at the western edge of a dense redwood forest. It is situated on a quiet tidal stretch of the river. You can often hear the surf crashing just a mile to the west. The roar intrudes upon but does not overcome the quiet of the campground.

Though there are many large redwoods here, there are even more old stumps, evidence of pioneer logging. Most of these have springboard cuts still showing on their eroded surfaces, indicating that the trees were cut before the introduction of chain saws. (The sawyers

---

RIVER TRAIL SOUTH:

DISTANCE: 1 mile round trip (connects with 1 1/4 mile headlands/beach trail).

TERRAIN: Down the river canyon, under the highway bridge, then climbing the bluff to grassy headlands.

BEST TIME: Spring for wildflowers but anytime is good.

WARNINGS: Watch for poison oak and stinging nettles.

DIRECTIONS TO TRAILHEAD: Turn east off Highway 1 at M.58.2 (Sonoma County), about .25 mile south of the town of Gualala. Go .7 mile to the campground, then .1 farther to its south end.

FURTHER INFO: Gualala Point Regional Park (707) 785-2377.

ENVIRONMENTAL CAMPS: 7 walk- or bike-in camps are located from 75 feet to 400 feet along the trail in a dense bay laurel forest near the river.

---

would stand on these springboards, five or ten feet above the ground to avoid cutting through the thicker, often scarred wood at the tree's base.) Many of these old stumps have new plants growing healthily from their tops. If you walk through the campground you will see the following plants atop stumps: elderberry, huckleberry, sword fern and bay laurel.

Where the redwood trees stop near the southwest end of the campground, bay laurels grow very large, with gnarled trunks up to four feet in diameter.

The river trail leads south through this dense bay laurel forest from the south end of the campground. Seven walk- or bike-in campsites are located in this forest along the first 400 feet of trail. (They are a bargain at $1 per night.) Just beyond the last campsite, the trail comes to a grassy clearing; a dense tangle of brush grows on your right, between you and the river.

At 1/8 mile the trail swings right and follows the river bank. It continues through tall brush for the next 1/16 mile, crossing a small wooden bridge, knocked askew by winter floods.

About 1/4 mile from the trailhead you pass under the highway bridge. Many cliff swallows nest under the bridge, especially on its west side. From March through September the swallows will be chattering and feeding over the river.

Your trail then leads uphill away from the river, following a fence. Then, passing an old snag, you leave the grassy river flat and climb the face of the bluff. The tangle of brush along the trail includes many species: willows, bay laurel, ceanothus, blackberries, wild rose, Indian paintbrush and poison oak. The trail switchbacks twice, coming to a bench where you may rest and enjoy the view.

As you come to the top of the bluff, the flora changes to bluff grassland, scattered with low cypress. Another 1/8 mile along the bluff's edge brings you to a pleasant picnic area. A few hundred feet beyond, you come to the visitor center. At this point you may return to the campground or continue to the network of headlands and beach trails (see Gualala Point Regional Park Headlands to Beach loop).

40.

SEA RANCH

SALAL TRAIL to BLUFFTOP TRAIL

This trail was mandated by state law in 1980, the resolution of years of litigation and lawsuits which went all the way to the Supreme Court. The Salal Trail is currently open. The Blufftop portion of the trail is scheduled to open in two stages. The section described below, from Salal Beach north, is due to open in November 1986. The 2 1/4 mile segment which leads south to Walk-on Beach has been delayed until 1987.

The Salal trail leads southeast from near the rest-room and parking area. It quickly becomes difficult to follow, not being well marked until beyond the golf clubhouse. Continue generally southeast along the south shoulder of the road to the park entrance on Highway 1. The vague track then parallels the highway south past two alternate parking spots for the next 1/10 mile.

A wooden post with blue lettering marks the point where the trail heads away from Highway 1. Go through a dense berry patch, then down a stairway

```
┌─────────────────────────────────────────┐
│                SEA RANCH:                 │
├─────────────────────────────────────────┤
│ DISTANCE: 2 1/2 miles round trip.         │
│ TERRAIN: Grassy headlands spotted with    │
│   cypress, then dropping into narrow,      │
│   wooded coastal creek canyon leading to   │
│   rocky beach. Then along the              │
│   spectacular coastal bluffs west of the   │
│   Sea Ranch subdivision.                   │
│ BEST TIME: Spring for the azaleas and      │
│   other wildflowers, but anytime is nice.  │
│ WARNINGS: Do not trespass on adjacent      │
│   private property. Watch for poison oak   │
│   along the trail. Be careful along the    │
│   crumbly blufftops. Stay on the trail     │
│   and away from the edge.                  │
│ DIRECTIONS TO TRAILHEAD: Turn west         │
│   from Highway 1 at M.58.2 (Sonoma         │
│   County) into the day use area for        │
│   Gualala Point Regional Park. Take the    │
│   first left inside the park, parking near │
│   the restrooms. Or you may park on the    │
│   west side of Highway 1 at M.58.10        │
│   (2-3 cars) or M.58.05 (1 car).           │
│ FURTHER INFO: Gualala Point Regional       │
│   Park (707) 785-2377.                     │
└─────────────────────────────────────────┘
```

into the creek canyon; you are 1/4 mile from the trailhead. This little creek canyon forms a habitat distinct from the coastal grasslands adjacent to it. Many species thrive in the cool, damp wind-protected environment including fragrant wild azalea, madrone, salal, alder, berries and oaks.

In 100 feet you cross a different trail; stay in the canyon, coming quickly to stands of redwoods, Bishop pines and droopy Douglas fir. You then come to a recent landfill, used to repair flood damage from the winter of '85-86. Just beyond is a small wooden bridge, then a paved road, 3/8 mile from the trailhead.

Cross the road along a faded double white line (used to mark trail crossings). Going southwest you pass another blue-lettered trail marker. The trail then comes back alongside the creek in an area lushly grown with willows, sword ferns, skunk cabbage and salmonberries. These are soon joined by Bishop pines and cypress.

At 1/2 mile from the trailhead cross a small bridge by wild azaleas, then plunge into a dense tunnel of growth dominated by oaks, alders and thimbleberries. In 1/16 mile you come to a more open portion of the trail. Indian paintbrush thrives in this rocky spot. Then you drop into another tunnel of brush, predominantly bay laurel.

Nearly 5/8 mile from the trailhead you come to a dense stand of redwoods on the creek. The trees are snapped off just above the level of the surrounding grasslands, attesting to the protection this little canyon provides from prevailing strong winds. This pretty spot has a small waterfall. Not far beyond you come to a muddy stretch of trail, still following the left side of the creek. In another 150 feet you find a dense salmonberry thicket on the right side of the trail. Salmonberries ripen in May and June. Then cross another paved path on a double white line. Miners lettuce grows on the far side of the path.

Not quite 3/4 mile from the trailhead a small rocky beach comes into view at the mouth of the creek. The wooded habitat gives way to soft chaparral plants: skunk cabbage, cow parsnip, horsetail ferns, grasses and assorted wildflowers.

The new Blufftop trail (to open November 1986) heads generally northwest from the junction, climbing steeply to the blufftop. Your trail crosses grassy headlands spotted with bush lupine, quickly meeting the rugged shoreline. You hug the shore, crossing two small gullies near the 1 mile point.

At 1 1/4 miles you pass through the first of several low cypress windrows which grow along the next section of shore. About 200 feet beyond is Gualala Point, shrouded in bushy cypress. Sea birds frequent Gualala Point Island, just offshore.

You then head northeast along the bluff's edge. At 1 3/8 miles the trail passes above a small, inaccessible pocket beach. Trail and shore jog left here and pass through a larger windrow. You come to a small point with unobstructed views south to Gualala Point and northwest to Whale Watch Point.

For the next 1/4 mile the nearby shore is mostly

hidden behind dense cypress. Recent grading and excavation mar the landscape on your right. At 1 3/4 miles you come to a fence where you enter Gualala Point Regional Park and meet the Headlands to Beach Loop trail. A right turn brings you to the Visitor Center in 1/4 mile. (You can go left for a longer blufftop hike.)

From the Visitor Center you must parallel the park road for 1/2 mile to return to the Salal trailhead and your car.

40A.

SEA RANCH
ALTERNATE TRAILS

THE SHELL BEACH TRAIL heads southeast through pines to a wooden bridge. Just short of 1/8 mile you cross a paved road, then continue over grasslands with scattered trees. About 1/4 mile from the trailhead you walk between houses on your left and right, then cross a second paved road. In 1/16 mile

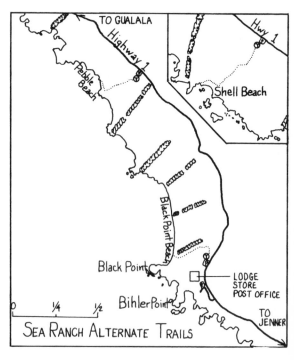

SEA RANCH ALTERNATE TRAILS

SEA RANCH ALTERNATE TRAILS:

DISTANCE: 1/2 mile to 1 1/4 miles round trip.

TERRAIN: Coastal grasslands leading to small pocket beaches.

BEST TIME: Spring for the wildflowers, low tide for best enjoyment of beaches and tide pools. Trails are nice anytime.

WARNINGS: Respect adjacent private property — do not trespass. All trails have a $1 per vehicle day use fee. Watch for rogue waves when on the beach. Trails are open 6 A.M. to 7 P.M.

DIRECTIONS TO TRAILHEADS: All on west side of Highway 1 at the following Sonoma County mileposts (just south of Gualala):

    Shell Beach Trail: M.55.20

    Pebble Beach Trail: M.52.30

    Black Point Beach Trail: M.51.40

Still to be developed are two similar trails:

    Walk-on Beach Trail: M.56.76

    Pocket Beach Trail: M.53.96

FURTHER INFO: Gualala Point Regional Park (707) 785-2377.

you come to a stairway to the pleasant beach, protected somewhat by the point to the north.

THE PEBBLE BEACH TRAIL heads south between shore pines. At 250 feet you cross a private path at a right angle. The trail then leads west through Bishop pines. On your right runs a lush creekbed, home to skunk cabbage, ferns and other water-loving plants. At 1/8 mile you leave the drainage for grassy headlands. At not quite 1/4 mile the trail follows along a cypress windbreak. You soon meet another private path, entering from the left. Go right here across a small wooden bridge. In another 150 feet you come to the stairway to Pebble Beach. The beach is gray, pebbly sand with good tide pools at low tide.

    Return by the same trail.

THE BLACK POINT BEACH TRAIL goes north across lush grassy headlands. At 1/16 mile you cross a private road. The trail turns west in 150 feet, heading directly toward the sea cliffs. At 3/16 mile you cross a private Sea Ranch trail, then come to a sturdy stairway which descends by 86 steps to the beach near its south end. To the south is Black Point, a rock outcrop with windblown cypress, long a landmark to navigators on both land and sea. To the north the black sand and pebbly beach extends about 1/2 mile. Return by the same trail.

CROSS REFERENCE LISTING

38. Headlands to Beach Loop
   Other trails may be handicapped accessible with assistance or for marginally handicapped.

TRAILS FOR JOGGERS

   9. North to Ten Mile River
   12. Glass Beach/Pudding Creek Headlands
   14. Mendocino Coast Botanical Gardens
   17-2. Mendocino Hiking & Equestrian Trail, Part 2
   24. Mendocino Hiking & Equestrian Trail, Part 3
   27. Chapman Point
   29. Van Damme State Park
   30. Navarro-By-The-Sea
   33. Navarro River Hike
   35. Manchester State Beach
   38. Headlands to Beach Loop
   40. Sea Ranch

CANOE ACCESS

   Eel River: Highway 1 at M.105.00
               Highway 101 at many points
   Ten Mile River: Highway 1 at M.69.65
   Lake Cleone: see trail #11.
   Noyo River: Near Fort Bragg. Access from North or South Harbor Drive or various logging roads.
   Big River: N. Big River Road at M.50.35.
   Albion River: Turn onto Albion River North Side Rd. at M.39.95.
   Navarro River: Trail #30 at M.40.15 or various points along Highway 128.
   Garcia River: Highway 1 at M.18.48 or from Miners Hole Road. (M.17.55)
   Gualala River: see trails #38 and #39, or from various side roads.

FAVORITE PLACES TO EAT ON THE COAST

   Cafe Beaujolais: Mendocino 937-5614
   Cap'n Flints: Noyo 964-9447
   D'Aurelio's: Fort Bragg 964-4227
   El Mexicano: Noyo 964-7164
   Floodgate Cafe: Navarro 895-2422
   Greenwood Pier Cafe: Elk 877-9997
   Gualala Hotel: Gualala 884-3441
   Lee's Chinese: Fort Bragg 964-6843
   Little River Restaurant: Little River 937-4945
   Lu's Bay Kitchen: Mendocino 937-0243
   Purple Rose: Cleone 964-6507
   The Restaurant: Fort Bragg 964-9800
   Wellspring: Mendocino 937-4567

COMMON & SCIENTIFIC NAMES OF PLANTS ALONG THE TRAILS

alyssum, *Lobularia maritima*

azalea (western azalea),
  Rhododendron occidentale

baby blue eyes, *Nemophila menziesii*

bay laurel, (Calif. bay, pepperwood),
  Umbellularia californica

beach morning glory,
  Calystegia soldanella

beach pea, *Lathyrus japonicus var. glaber*

beach primrose,
  Oenothera cheiranthifolia

beach strawberry, *Fragaria chiloensis*

bear grass,
  Xerophyllum tenax

big leaf maple,
  Acer macrophyllum

bird's foot fern (bird's foot cliff brake, poison fern),
  Pellaea mucronata

Bishop pine, *Pinus muricata*

black twinberry,
  Lonicera involucrata

blueblossom (Calif. lilac),
  Ceanothus thyrsiflorus

blue dick,
  Dichelostemma pulchellum

blue-eyed grass,
  Sisyrinchium sp.

blue gum eucalyptus,
  Eucalyptus globulus

Bolander pine,
  Pinus contorta ssp. bolanderi

bracken fern, *Pteridium aquilinum var. pubescens*

brodiaea (tall brodiaea),
  Brodiaea laxa

buttercup,
  Ranunculus californicus

California nutmeg,
  Torreya californica

California poppy (golden poppy),
  Eschscholtzia californica

* calla lily, *Zantedeschia aethiopica*

calypso orchid,
  Calypso bulbosa

canyon live oak,
  Quercus chrysolepis

cascara sagrada,
  Rhamnus purshiana

cattail, *Typha sp.*

chamise,
  Adenostoma fasciculatum

chicks and hens,
  Dudleya farinosa

chinquapin,
  Chrysolepis chrysophylla

clintonia,
  Clintonia andrewsiana

coast buckwheat,
  Eriogonum latifolium

coast lily, *Lilium maritimum*

coastal manroot (wild cucumber),
  Marah oreganus

columbine,
  Aquilegia formosa

common iceplant (sea fig),
  Mesembryathemum sp.

corn lily,
Veratrum fimbriatum

* cotoneaster, Cotoneaster sp.

cow parsnip,
Heracleum lanatum

* creeping myrtle, Vinca minor

cypress. Cupressus sp.

dandelion,
Taraxacum officinale

deer fern, Blechnum spicant

Douglas fir,
Pseudotsuga menziesii

Douglas iris,
Iris douglasiana

elderberry,
Sambucus callicarpa

evergreen huckleberry
(Calif. huckleberry),
Vaccinium ovatum

evergreen violet
(redwood violet),
Viola sempervirens

fairy bells, Disporum smithii

false lily of the valley,
Maianthemum dilatum

false solomon's seal,
Smilacina racemosa

filaree (scissors grass,
redstem storksbill),
Erodium cicutarium

five finger fern (maidenhair
fern), Adiantum pedatum
var. aleuticum

Fort Bragg manzanita (dwarf
manzanita),
Arctostaphylos
nummularia

* foxglove, Digitalis purpurea

giant chain fern,
Woodwardia fimbriata

giant horsetail,
Equisetum telmateia

godetia (farewell to spring),
Clarkia sp.

gold back fern (stamp fern),
Pityrogramma
triangularis

* gorse, Ulex europaeus

grand fir, Abies grandis

gum plant, Grindelia stricta

hairy manzanita,
Arctostaphylos
columbiana

Himalayan blackberry,
Rubus procerus

horehound,
Marrubium vulgare

horsetail, Equisetum sp.

huckleberry, Vaccinium sp.

iceplant,
Mesembryanthemum sp.

Indian paintbrush,
Castilleja sp.

Indian warrior,
Pedicularis densiflora

knobcone pine,
Pinus attenuata

Labrador tea,
Ledum glandulosum
var. columbianum

ladies' tresses,
Spiranthus romanzoffiana

lady fern,
Athyrium filix-femina
var. sitchenense

laurel,
Umbellularia californica

leather fern
(leather leaf fern),
Polypodium scouleri

leopard lily,
Lilium pardalinum

licorice fern,
Polypodium glycyrrhiza

live-forever, *Dudleya sp*.

lupine, *Lupinus latifolius, L.*
littoralis, L. nanus,
L. polyphyllus,
L. variicolor, L. rivularis

madrone, *Arbutus menziesii*

manzanita,
Arctostaphylos sp.

Mendocino cypress,
Cupressus pygmaea

miners lettuce,
Montia sibirica

monkey flower,
Mimulus guttatus
ssp. litoralis

Monterey cypress, *Cupressus*
macrocarpa

narcissus,
Amaryllidaceae sp.

nasturtium (Indian cress),
Tropaeolum sp.

nettle, *Urtica sp*.

one leaved wild onion,
Allium unifolium

Oregon grape,
Mahonia nervosa

Pacific dogwood,
Cornus nuttallii

Pacific waterleaf,
Hydrophyllum tenuipes

paintbrush,
Castilleja latifolia,
C. affinis, C. foliolosa,
C. hololeuca, C. wightii,
C. mendosensis

* pampas grass,
Cortaderia selloana

pig-a-back plant
(piggyback),
Tolmiea menziesii

plantain, *Plantago sp*.

poison hemlock,
Conium maculatum

poison oak,
Toxicodendron
diversiloba

poppy,
Eschscholzia californica

* Port Orford cedar,
Chamaecyparis
lawsoniana

raspberry,
Rubus leucodermis

red alder, *Alnus rubra*

red clover,
Trifolium pratense

* red hot poker,
Kniphofia uvaria

red huckleberry, *Vaccinium*
parvifolium

redwood,
Sequoia sempervirens

redwood lily,
Lilium rubescens

redwood sorrel,
Oxalis oregana

rein orchid,
Habenaria elegans
var. maritima

rhododendron (Calif. rose
bay), *Rhododendron*
macrophyllum

rush, *Juncus sphaerocarpus*

salal, *Gaultheria shallon*

salmonberry,
Rubus spectabilis

sand verbena, yellow,
Abronia latifolia

sand verbena, pink, *Abronia*
umbellata

* Scotch broom,
Cytisus scoparius

scouring rush,
Equisetum hyemale

scrub oak, *Quercus dumosa*
var. bullata engelmann

seaside daisy,
    Erigeron glaucus

sea thrift, *Armeria maritima
    var. californica*

sedge, *Carex sp.*

shore pine, *Pinus contorta
    ssp. contorta*

silverweed, *Potentilla egedei
    var. grandis*

Sitka spruce,
    Picea sitchensis

skunk cabbage,
    Lysichitum americanum

slink pod
    (fetid adders tongue),
    Scoliopus bigelovii

* spearmint, *Mentha spicata*

sphagnum moss,
    Sphagnum sp.

starflower,
    Trientalis latifolia

sticky monkeyflower
    (bush monkeyflower),
    Mimulus aurantiacus

stinging nettle, *Urtica lyalli*

sundew,
    Drosera rotundifolia

sword fern
    (western sword fern),
    Polystichum munitum

tanoak,
    Lithocarpus densiflorus

thimbleberry,
    Rubus parviflorus

thistle, *Cirsium brevistylum*

trillium (wake robin),
    Trillium chloropetalum,
    T. ovatum

vanilla leaf (deer foot),
    Achlys triphylla

vetch, *Vicia angustifolia*

vine maple, *Acer circinatum*

wax myrtle (bayberry),
    Myrica californica

western hemlock,
    Tsuga heterophylla

western windflower,
    Anemone deltoidea

whitethorn,
    Ceanothus incanus

wild ginger,
    Asarum caudatum

wild mustard,
    Brassica campestris

wild rose, *Rosa sp.*

willow, *Salix sp.*

wintergreen, *Pyrola sp.*

wood fern, *Dryopteris arguta*

woodwardia fern (giantfern),
    Woodwardia fimbriata

yarrow, *Achillea millefolium*

yerba de selva (modesty),
    Whipplea modesta

* *Introduced species*

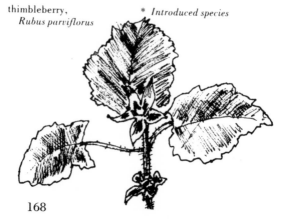

168

BIBLIOGRAPHY

Adams, Rick and Louise McCorkle, *The California Highway 1 Book*, Ballantine Books, New York, 1985.

Alt, David D. and Donald W. Hyndman, *Roadside Geology of Northern California*, Mountain Press Publishing Co., Missoula, Montana, 1975.

Bear, Dorothy and Beth Stebbins, *Mendocino Book One*, Mendocino Historical Research, Inc., Mendocino, Ca., 1973.

Bear, Dorothy and Beth Stebbins, *A Tour of Mendocino*, Mendocino Historical Research, Inc., Mendocino, Ca., 1970.

Becking, Rudolph, *Pocket Flora of the Redwood Forest*, Island Press, Covelo, Ca., 1982.

Borden, Stanley, California Western Railroad, *Western Railroader*, Vol. 20, #8, San Mateo, Ca., 1965.

Borden, Stanley, Caspar Lumber Company, *Western Railroader*, Issues 315-316, San Mateo, Ca.

California Coastal Access Guide, University of California Press, Berkeley, 1983.

Carpenter, Aurelius, *History of Mendocino County*, Pacific Rim Press, Mendocino, Ca., reprint of 1914 edition.

Dewitt, John B., *California Redwood Parks and Preserves*, Save-the-Redwoods League, San Francisco, 1982.

Grillos, Steve J., *Ferns and Fern Allies of California*, University of California Press, Berkeley, 1966.

Hayden, Mike, *Exploring the North Coast*, Chronicle Books, San Francisco, 1982.

Hyman, Frank J., *Historic Writings*, self-published, Fort Bragg, Ca., 1966.

Jackson, Walter A., *The Doghole Schooners*, Bear & Stebbins, Mendocino, Ca., 1977.

Jenny, Hans, *The Pygmy Forest Ecological Staircase*, Nature Conservancy, 1973.

Keator, Glenn and Ruth Heady, *Pacific Coast Berry Finder*, Nature Study Guild, Berkeley, 1978.

Keator, Glenn and Ruth Heady, *Pacific Coast Fern Finder*, Nature Study Guild, Berkeley, 1981.

Kroeber, A.L., *Handbook of the Indians of California*, Dover Publications, New York, 1976.

Levene, Bruce and William Bradd, Lana Krasner, Gloria Petrykowski, Rosalie Zucker, *Mendocino County Remembered: An Oral History, Volumes I and II*, Mendocino County Historical Society, 1980.

McConnaughey, Bayard H. and Evelyn McConnaughey, *Pacific Coast*, Audubon Society Nature Guides, Alfred A. Knopf, New York, 1985.

Mendocino Coastal Research Group, *Mendocino Coast: A Vanishing Resource*, Western Interstate Commission for Higher Education, 1972.

169

Mendocino Historical Review, Volume IV, Number 4, Summer 1978, Mendocino Historical Research, Inc., Mendocino, Ca.

Mendocino Historical Review, Volume IX, Number I, Spring 1986, Mendocino Historical Research Inc., Mendocino, Ca.

Munz, Philip A., *California Spring Wildflowers*, University of California Press, Berkeley, 1961.

Munz, Philip A., *Shore Wildflowers of California, Oregon and Washington*, University of California Press, Berkeley, 1973.

Niehaus, Theodore F. and Charles L. Ripper, *Field Guide to Pacific States Wildflowers*, (Peterson Field Guide Series) Houghton Mifflin, Boston, 1976.

Randall, Warren R., Robert F. Keniston and Dale N. Bever, *Manual of Oregon Trees and Shrubs*, Oregon State University Bookstores, Corvallis, Or., 1978.

Russo, Ron and Pam Olhausen, *Pacific Intertidal Life*, Nature Study Guild, Berkeley, 1981.

Ryder, David W., *Memories of the Mendocino Coast*, Taylor and Taylor, 1948.

Sholars, Robert, *The Pygmy Forest and Associated Plant Communities of Coastal Mendocino County, California*, self-published, Mendocino, Ca., 1982.

Watts, Phoebe, *Redwood Region Flower Finder*, Nature Study Guild, Berkeley, 1979.

Watts, Tom, *Pacific Coast Tree Finder*, Nature Study Guild, Berkeley, 1973.

Wurm, Ted, Caspar, South Fork and Eastern Railroad, *Short and Narrow Rails*, July 1979, Volume 2, Number 1.

Young, Dorothy King, *Redwood Empire Wildflowers*, Third Edition, Naturegraphs Publishers, Happy Camp, Ca., 1976.

INDEX

BORED FEET PUBLICATIONS

offers a fine selection of books, maps and posters about California's North Coast/Redwood Empire. Your purchase from Bored Feet supports independent publishing. In return we will keep you informed about the latest and greatest publications about this spectacular scenic area.

BOOKS OF GENERAL INTEREST

The Hiker's Hip Pocket Guide to the Mendocino Coast, $9.95
Lorentzen. The Coast's first and only trail guide.

California Highway 1 Book, Adams & McCorkle. 17.95
Definitive guide to this breathtaking highway.

California Coastal Access Guide, Official guide to 10.95
public access for entire California coast.

Redwood Empire, Collings. Color overview of the 14.95
unique redwood region.

Roadside Geology of Northern California, Alt & 9.95
Hyndman. Field guide to the rocks and road cuts.

Exploring the North Coast, Hayden. From Golden 8.95
Gate to Oregon line. Limited copies.

NATURE GUIDES

Audubon Society Nature Guides:
   Pacific Coast, McConnaughey. 14.95
   Western Forests, Whitney. 14.95
Pocket Flora of the Redwood Forest, Becking. 15.00
California Spring Wildflowers, Munz. 8.95
Shore Wildflowers of California, Oregon & 5.95
   Washington, Munz.
Pygmy Forest, Sholars. 6.95
Pacific Coast Tree Finder 1.50
Pacific Coast Fern Finder 1.50
Pacific Coast Berry Finder 1.50
Pacific Coast Bird Finder 1.50
Pacific Intertidal Life 1.50
Redwood Region Flower Finder 1.50
Plants Used by the Indians of Mendocino County 3.00
Abalone Book, Howarth. All about it. 5.95
Mushrooms Demystified, Arora. The complete west 24.95
coast fungus guide, 1000 pages, paper.

LOCAL HISTORY

Mendocino, Book One, Bear & Stebbins. Complete 8.95
history of the town, old photos, newly revised.

Tour of Mendocino, Bear & Stebbins. Self-guided 2.50
walking tour of the town, newly revised.

Noyo, Bear & Stebbins. Hot off the press! The little 13.95
known history of fishing village.

Mallets of the Mendocino Coast, Wurm. Fall 1986. 28.95
Complete story of Caspar Railroad, great photos.

Logging the Redwoods, Carranco & Labbe. Story of 17.95
the pioneer loggers of giants, many photos.

Redwood Classic, Andrews. Paperback history of 12.95
the falling of the giants.

Sentinels of Solitude, Gibbs. Paperback history of 9.95
west coast lighthouses.

Lighthouses of the Pacific, Gibbs. Cloth. Definitive   29.95
   guide to west coast lighthouses.

Mendocino County Remembered, Vol. I, Levene et   8.50
   al. Oral histories of Mendocino's pioneers.

Mendocino Past and Present. Collection of articles,   5.00
   old and new photos.

Books by Ray Raphael, chronicler of north coast history.
   An Everyday History of Somewhere   8.00
   Tree Talk. The people and politics of timber.   12.00
   Cash Crop. The people and politics of pot.   8.00

LOCAL COOKBOOKS

Cafe Beaujolais, Fox & Bear.   paper   9.95
   The Coast's most famous restaurant.   cloth   17.95
Favorite Seafood Recipes, Noyo Fishermen's Wives.   8.95
Mendocino Cookery, Levene.   6.50
Mendocino Coast Cooking, Levene.   6.95
Bahl Gorms in Boont, Sanders. In boontling.   4.00

MAPS

Metzger Mendocino County   5.00
Redwood Empire — Sonoma, Mendocino,   1.75
   Humboldt & Del Norte Counties.

POSTERS

Flowers of the Redwood Forest, L&D Klein.   7.95
Coastal Wildflowers of Northern Calif., L&D Klein.   7.95
Spring Wildflowers, Calif. Native Plant Society.   7.95
Shrubs of the Coast Range, Ca. Native Plant Society. 7.95

HOW TO ORDER

For shipping to an address in California, please add 6% sales tax. Out of state pays no sales tax.
For orders under $15.00, add 75¢ postage and handling.
For orders over $15.00, add $1.50 postage and handling.
Send your check or money order payable to Bored Feet Publications. We mail within 10 days. Orders sent book post unless you specify otherwise. Add $2.00 more for rush or special handling (UPS, overseas, etc.). We will promptly inform you of backorder. Specify if no back order.

ORDER FORM   Minimum order $6.00.

QTY	ITEM	PRICE	TOTAL
	6% Sales Tax	Shipping	
		TOTAL	

Please print clearly. Prices subject to change without notice.

NAME: _____

ADDRESS: _____

BORED FEET PUBLICATIONS
Post Office Box 1832, Mendocino, California 95460